# WANDERING HONG KONG WITH SPIRITS

## 和幽靈一起的香港漫遊

# WANDERING HONG KONG WITH SPIRITS
## 和幽靈一起的香港漫遊

Selected Poetry of **Liu Waitong**
## 廖偉棠 詩選

*Translated from the Chinese by* Enoch Yee-lok Tam, Desmond Sham,
Audrey Heijns, Chan Lai-kuen and Cao Shuying

Zephyr Press | **mccm**creations

Published in 2016 by
Zephyr Press    www.zephyrpress.org
MCCM Creations   www.mccmcreations.com

Cover and interior photographs by Liu Waitong
Book design by *type*slowly
Printed in Hong Kong

This title is part of the Hong Kong Atlas, a series of contemporary Hong Kong writing in English translation. Funded primarily by the HKADC's Literature Translation Project, and coordinated by the Faculty of Arts at Baptist University, these works include a broad range of poetry, prose and graphic adaptions from established and emerging Hong Kong authors.

The publishers acknowledge with gratitude the financial and administrative support of the Hong Kong Arts Development Council, the Massachusetts Cultural Council and the Faculty of Arts at Baptist University.

massculturalcouncil.org

香港浸會大學
HONG KONG BAPTIST UNIVERSITY

The Hong Kong Arts Development Council fully supports freedom of artistic expression. The views and opinions expressed in this project do not represent the stand of the Council.

Supported by

香港藝術發展局
Hong Kong Arts Development Council

*Cataloguing-in publication data is available from the Library of Congress.*

ISBN 978-1-938890-03-1 (US)
ISBN 978-988-13115-3-5 (HK)

# CONTENTS

# Preface

"I'm a 49-year-old pier shaking my head in the cold,
shaking my head I touch the wound between my ribs, I watch
government bastards rub their hands,
shaking my head as the screaming gulls count my bones"

—*Ballad of the Central Star Ferry Pier, Liu Waitong*

Hong Kong has long existed in some unknown future tense. Its history—from at least the mid-1800s until today—is a complex narrative of emigration and trade, which has resulted in a society now scrambling to make sense of perpetual waves of dislocation. This is an isolated rootlessness that ends primarily not in a nostalgic form of roots seeking, but in a practical search for employment, personal meaning and private space among the shifting urban corridors.

The 2006 demolition of the Star Ferry clock tower, followed by the 2008 destruction of Queen's Pier, launched Hong Kong's modern heritage movement. The erasure of Queen's Pier literally no longer stands as testament to the decades of ceremonial arrivals and departures from Victoria Harbor. Dismantled by the government in the name of land reclamation, the high-level ceremonies surrounding the pier (named for Queen Victoria) resonated with a strong colonial component, which was likely a much greater factor in its destruction than any practical need to redevelop the pier. Historical memory becomes considerably simpler to efface when a landscape is inexorably changed.

Some of the most compelling of Hong Kong's contemporary writers actively engage with these foundational issues of urbanization and heritage loss, as well as with the inherent bizarreness of daily life that is created in the process. The poet and photographer Liu Waitong 廖偉棠 deals precisely with these and related issues of critical impact on today's

Hong Kong and mainland China, while referencing and elegizing a host of cultural influences. One of the more celebrated of Hong Kong poets of his and earlier generations, Liu Waitong has received numerous literary awards in Hong Kong and Taiwan, including the Hong Kong Chinese Literature Award, the China Times Literature Award and the United Daily News Literature Award. The author of more than eight poetry collections, he is also an established photographer who has shown internationally.

Liu Waitong was born in Guangdong in 1975 and emigrated to Hong Kong in 1997. In the early 2000s, he then moved to Beijing for several years before returning to Hong Kong. Within these peripatetic movements he has simultaneously become "of Hong Kong," while maintaining a vestige of "the other." One ear is always pressed back to the Mainland, considering and commenting on Hong Kong's rapid transformation:

> 5,000 years from now the water line
> will rise to Des Voeux and Johnston Roads,
> sea otters and rats will make hundreds of holes in the frame of
> the half-flooded new wing of the HKCEC, more than a thousand holes
> in the IFC. The rain will be constant.
> An umbrella will be unearthed in the rubble of the Legislative Council

> *—The Future History of Hong Kong Island*

Written well before Hong Kong's 2014 Occupy Movement, the unearthed umbrella becomes hauntingly prescient. At least 25% of Hong Kong's developed area exists on reclaimed land and, as Victoria Harbor continues to shrink, generations from now either will be able to stroll a short bridge from Hong Kong Island to Kowloon, or else the shifting climate will have taken back the land, so that the umbrella will join a flotilla of survivors heading back up the Pearl River Delta searching for fresh water and land to develop. What was lost on many Western commentators in 2014, is that the vague concept of "Democracy" was less important than the protestors' real concerns with housing, loss of heritage and language, and some semblance of control over their city's evolution.

In late 2014, China's State Administration for Press, Publication, Radio, Film and Television ordered Chinese media outlets to crack down on the use of puns and "irregular" Chinese in programming—stating that the practice of tweaking idioms within the "pure" Chinese language would lead to cultural and linguistic chaos. Within this newish world order, Liu Waitong's writing and photography are fluid artifacts that gain a sense of precision through their liminal space, situated somewhere between Hong Kong and the Mainland. His vessels become dance partners in the shrinking Victoria harbor, and there is an ever present—but never all-consuming—sense of estrangement, fueled by the split between his dueling identities. Liu Waitong is often viewed within the tradition of those Mainland writers who variously fled, or wandered, across the border beginning in the 1920s and '30s, and his regular movement back and forth has assisted in him becoming an acute observer of society on both sides of the barbed wire.

These travels can also lead to moments of linguistic espionage and a sense of being trapped between societies, as in his poem on watching a July 1st Hong Kong protest from the confines of Beijing—"I've been detained by another city, each day letting myself grow possessed by its sweet words." The author is torn between the boundless opportunities available in Beijing's new artistic and cultural hubs, and the memory of his own participation at recent protests back in Hong Kong. "I open the windows, and my mouth immediately fills up with debris from the new world." It's then through his writing that he is able to transform debris into stanzas that lay bare his divided self.

Much of Liu Waitong's writing is dimly lit, blurred by train lines and the elements. Within these settings, the author grasps for concepts to ground what is both fleeting and hazily drawn through various eras:

We are like a young McDull, happily cramming
onto a wingless tram, driving into a mountain wrapped in weeds,
leaves and branches not yet stretched in our sleeves
as the peak fog swoops, flooding across.

We are like negative equity sinking a middle-aged McDull.
Drunken Taiping peak, 9/11 in the fog belongs
to you—wax figures dashing under the light of a fire brigade,
hastily delivering us contorted wine bottles, telescopes for old age.

       *—Fog Taiping Shan Peak*

McDull, the hapless and beloved children's character, navigates readers through the upper reaches of Hong Kong Island, where up until 1940, native Chinese were not allowed to live without express approval from the Governor-in-Council. The opening stanza is constituted by vines and swatches of green, in place of the ubiquitous housing developments that now dot Victoria Peak. Then in the following lines, the post-post-misty mountains are replaced by the aging animated pig pondering his dwindling savings and the aftermath of the Word Trade Center attacks. The "telescopes for old age" peer back onto Kowloon, which remain solidly affixed to the Mainland, while glacially shifting northwards as part of the reunification scheme.

Within this maelstrom of socio-political movements, it is vital to note that Liu Waitong should not be branded primarily as a political poet; rather, his writing and photographs touch on any number of key issues concerning Hong Kong's landscape that are inherently political. This gray area is a key to entering his work. Liu Waitong is a careful observer. If pressed to give a single moniker to his writing, I would refer to him as a poet of longing—of past eras, former loves, lost neighborhoods and poetic mentors. Though his most recent book of poetry and photographs— *Umbrella-topia*—will likely shift the reading public's gaze back to his more politically leaning tendencies.

More so than the shifting space of national boundaries, Waitong's poetry is unsettled by eras, never wholly comfortable in the present. His is a constant struggle to remember without allowing nostalgia to enter and completely blur the lines. In his poem to the celebrated Mainland/Hong Kong writer Dai Wangshu, "Looking for Woodbrook Villa on Pokfulam Road," Waitong becomes "silent as a dog whose scent has been washed away by the rain." Within the poem the search for Dai Wangshu's old residence becomes a platform for Liu Waitong to place himself within a lineage of authors who have lived a similarly hybrid existence. Along the way, any trace of an originary point has been scuttled, either by the elements or through a host of interwoven factors. The photographs scattered throughout this volume give further form to his affinity for erasure by shadow, where he is able to divine the outlines of forms against a Hong Kong backdrop of glass and metal angles. Or, more correctly, his words are reflected back to the reader in these constructed angles.

★ ★ ★

As with any volume of translation, there are myriad levels of complexity to consider. This project was further complicated by the shear volume of Liu Waitong's writing, along with the number of translators who had been collaborating with him over the past decade. In a few cases, two or more translators were working simultaneously from "anonymous" draft English-language translations, and a considerable amount of sleuthing was employed to trace each draft back to its original translator. Thankfully, a majority of the poems in this volume were translated specifically for the book.

Enoch Yee-lok Tam, Desmond Sham and Audrey Heijns are owed a tremendous debt of gratitude for their work in helping to create and to edit this representative selection. Just like Charlie in Liu Waitong's ode to the night market on Temple Street, their work "uncovers the miracle of each place." And by following Liu Waitong down these alleys—along with his editors and translators—English-language readers now have access to the Hong Kong markets and warehouse spaces where he has been collecting his sharp fragments of words.

Sincere thanks also are due to the Hong Kong Arts Development Council (HKADC), which is the primary funder for this and other books in the Hong Kong Atlas series. The HKADC-funded project will make available, in print and digital formats, bilingual collections of poetry, as well as fiction and graphic adaptations of contemporary Hong Kong literature. Authors in the series include a mix of established and emerging voices, ranging from classic untranslated works such as Ng Hui-bin's *The Bisons* and Leung Ping-kwan's *Paper Cut-outs* to a new generation of writers—Hon Lai Chu, Dung Kai-cheung, Tse Dorothy Hiu-hung, and Natalia Chan. Hong Kong Atlas—which borrows its name from the Dung Kai-cheung novel—is an important first step in expanding the English-language canon with a range of Hong Kong voices. By drawing on literature, translation and creative culture as a way of remapping a global city, the Atlas project offers alternative histories to Hong Kong through its own literature. Hong Kong gets to speak for itself.

—*Christopher Mattison, June 2015, Hong Kong*

# 窗前樹

風過時它便翻動一身的銀和綠，
去年如此，今年如此。
十年前它也許更為逍遙，
在蘇州街一些平房中間，
那些平房裏住了一些學生
和中關村最早的賣盜版的婦女，
那些樸素的情侶和自得其樂的母子
黃昏時會在樹下嬉戲。
誰也沒多考慮未來的新世界
將會怎樣撥弄他們的命運，
這些人、這棵樹。

風過時它便翻動一身的銀和綠，
去年如此，今年如此。
前年蘇州街北口完全變成了一個工地，
地產商帶來了建材、民工和簡易棚屋
鏟平了舊房子和寧靜的生活。
奇怪的是大樹還留著，
還越來越高大、茂密，
只是身上多了一兩根拉長的繩子
掛著民工們的汗衣。
前年冬天我剛搬到蘇州街，
去年春天我才第一次留意這樹：
民工們晚上愛在樹下喝酒、默坐，
後來還有一些拾荒者在樹下擺攤，
買給他們一些城市的破爛。
到夏天，我漸漸能越過工地的噪音
單獨聽到樹葉子的沙沙聲。

# Tree outside the Window

The wind blows, rustling through silver and green,
last year, like this year.
A decade ago it was more free to wander
among the houses on Suzhou Street where students lived
and women hawked pirated discs from Zhongguancun,
austere lovers, mothers and sons content
to play around the tree at dusk.
No one considers how the future's new world
will affect their fate,
these people, this tree.

The wind blows, rustling through silver and green,
last year, like this year.
Two years ago the north of Suzhou Street turned construction site,
property developers hauling in materials, workers and sheds,
shoveling away the old houses and tranquil life.
For some odd reason the enormous tree was spared,
growing larger, bushier,
a couple of ropes lashed to its trunk
for hanging up workers' shirts.
Two years ago this winter I moved to Suzhou Street,
not noticing the tree until last spring:
workers at night sat and drank silently beneath.
Later, scavengers would set up stalls
for the city's scraps.
By summer, I learned to block out the construction noise,
and listen all on my own to the rustling leaves.

今年那些新大廈紛紛落成，
還記得舊時光的，只有
這棵樹和我住的蘇州街二號樓。
窗前的工地慢慢變成一個樓盤，
有中產階級喜歡的珠光寶氣和升值可能。
我也明白了地產商為何有留下此樹的仁慈
——樹的旁邊將建成一個私有的園圃，
為這"家園"更添一些售賣價值。
蘇州街二號樓和我，也將被新世界拆除，
新世界又將被更新的世界替代。
這首詩裏最後只剩下這棵樹
風過時它便翻動一身的銀和綠。

This year new buildings are being completed,
I can still remember back when all that stood
was the tree and where I lived at No. 2 Suzhou Street.
The construction site outside my window gradually transforms into
                 a housing complex,
adorned in lavish jewels, which the middle-class adores.
I realize now why the developers benevolently saved the tree—
to build a private garden around,
upping the home's value.
No. 2 Suzhou Street and I will be discarded by a new world,
to be replaced by a newer world.
Only the tree in this poem will remain,
rustling through silver and green.

# 春夜又占貓詩一首

這夜仍有寂寞，是你。
聽不見昨夜雨，再冷一次。
你是寧靜海，北京動蕩著，槐花遍地。

不要再叫我，我在沿一根蛛絲攀援。
你是夜游神，半夜突然起來
吃我的夢：那些揚州路、西北劫。

不要再叫我，我是春夜拾花人。
和你一起走下故宮廢池，
水已深深，貓兒你得閉眼。

我若笑了，我便是鬼魂小兒
騎你入夜，一朵榆錢中，仰頭向她
一個鬼臉——屏息著，你是寧靜海，

圓頭小男孩。我也曾夜半驚呼
不得應。北京美，似大亂將至。
我們走南向北去——
化身千萬億，
讓她看不過來。這寂寞
隨風長大——

你是虎，與這春夜匹配。

# Another Divining Cat Poem, on a Spring Night

Tonight's loneliness, you.
Unable to hear last night's rain, it's turned cold again.
You're a tranquil sea, turbulent Beijing, fallen pagoda flowers.

Stop distracting me, I'm scaling a spider-silk thread.
You're a nighthawk, waking suddenly at midnight
to feed on my dreams: those Yangzhou roads, Northwest calamities.

Stop distracting me, I'm a flower-picker on a spring night.
Walking with you to an abandoned pond in the Forbidden City,
the water runs deep, please close your eyes, my little cat.

If I laughed, I'd be a young ghost
riding you at nightfall, with elm fruit, staring up into her
ghoul's face—holding a breath. You're a tranquil sea,

a round-headed boy. I scream out late at night
with no response. Beijing is lovely, a discontent is nearing.
We traipse from south to north—
incarnating into countless millions,
too many for her to grasp. This loneliness
grows with the wind—

You're a tiger, a good match for this spring night.

# 春光曲

我們已經熬過這個冬天，
聽到了滿天雪花掌聲雷動，
它們應該如此鼓掌歡送，
就像四年前的歡迎。

我在這一刻才真正感到惡心，
城市吞下了自己的兒子，
正當那兒子趴在天橋上
把舊雪、發票和假證如湯暢飲。

祝你們有個好胃口哪！
把能吃的東西都舔個干淨，
別忘了橋下賣報的那幾個下崗工人，
更別遺漏躲進裙底的那個大款。

春光已經熊熊，
為這麻辣火鍋加溫。
塗上了香水的豬們已經在暢泳，
到底哪些人能成為鍋裡的鴛鴦？

沒有用，即使你雇佣民工
在樓梯上向我贈送豪宅也沒有用。
我突然回頭走進內心的黑暗，
為那熄滅的一段光陰痛哭。

# A Song of Spring Light

We've survived winter,
heard snowflakes fill the sky with thunderous applause,
they should applaud when sending it off,
just like it was welcomed in four years ago.

Not until this moment do I feel the disgust,
when the city swallows its son,
as a child lies on the pedestrian bridge
drinking old snow out of invoices and forged papers.

I wish you bon appétit!
Eat everything you can and lick it all clean,
don't forget the laid-off workers hawking papers under the bridge,
or the tycoon hiding himself beneath a skirt.

Spring light already fierce and bright,
adds heat to a spicy hot-pot.
Pigs infused with perfume swim delightfully,
but who'll become the mandarin ducks in the pot?

There's no point offering me a luxury flat here on the stairs,
even if you can hire peasant workers, there's no point.
I turn abruptly to the darkness in my heart,
wailing over the fading time.

我為這個或那個城市痛哭，
它們抽出了細花和嫩葉也不能叫我稍留。
空中的一掌突然擊向我自己，
它認出了我是那個愛漂亮的農民。

我穿著灰領子狗做的西服，
打扮成白領子狗的模樣，
我的袖口卻露出了我媽繡的花邊，
情不自禁伸了伸雪白的翅膀。

我竭力飛起來為這春光痛哭，
一汪春水從我傷口中泛濫，
仿佛一個艷麗欲燃的翠湖，
我曾經在那裡歌唱，直到獵人開槍。

今夜我一個人穿越干燥的中國，
它干燥而且寒冷，在金乞衣裡叫窮，
吞下了自己的兒子。而窗外春月照澈，
全城的人都睡了，碎了，

明月對他們太重，不能入夢。

I wail over this or that city,
proffering delicate flowers and budding leaves won't keep me.
A fist raised in the air punches at me with no warning,
having recognized me as a vain peasant.

I wear Western suits made by grey-collar dogs,
dressed like a white-collar dog,
I can't refrain from stretching out my snow-white wings,
with lace borders on cuffs sewn by my mother.

I strain to fly, wailing over spring light,
a pool of spring water flows from my wound,
like a green lake, gaudy and blazing,
I once sang out until a hunter shot.

Tonight I alone cut across China's arid expanse,
cold and dry, like a beggar cloaked in gold, pleading poverty,
swallowing its own son. Yet the spring moon shines transparent
                    past the window,
the city's people have fallen asleep, shattered,

the moon is too heavy for them to fall into dreams.

# 凌晨4點，和我做愛

——給疏影

凌晨4點很快來臨，
每一天。而今天的缺失
是未來多少年後漫長的缺失的預演
（那時，我不在了，你在。
或者，你不在了，我在。）
一如這羅伯特·弗蘭克的黑白寶麗來照片。
但是，也許我們只是老了，變得更神秘
像這張照片裡的June，在凌晨4點
陌生旅館，50歲，赤裸，揚手，叉腰，
仿佛是跳起了弗羅明戈，在光芒中表情嚴肅。
"和我做愛吧，"和我做愛，羅伯特說。
凌晨4點帶來更大片的光芒，1979年
天一早就亮了。那是你出生的一年。
讓我們倒鏡頭：羅伯特的兒子長大、成為嬉皮、死亡，
羅伯特結婚、離婚、再結婚，
他鎖起徠卡相機、拿起電影攝影機、最後只用寶麗來，
"寶麗來——倏忽即逝去的，
影像的逐漸褪去——它們同生命本身一樣反抗保存"
你在筆記裡這樣寫道，你寫羅伯特·弗蘭克
因為他晚年的照片無一不使你落淚，
你也已經體驗戀愛、分手、再戀愛、再分手，
最後和我結婚，你繼續寫詩、寫童話、
拍針孔照片，許下10個新諾言，
你離家出走過、翻宿舍牆夜奔過、在北京和廣州迷過路，

# 4am, Make Love to Me

*—for Shuying*

It'll soon be 4am,
every day. And today's deficiency
is a rehearsal for a long string of deficiencies at some future time
(And, at that time, I won't be, but you will.
Or, you won't be, but I will.)
like Robert Frank's black and white Polaroids.
But, perhaps we only grow older and more mysterious,
like June in the photo, 4am,
in a foreign hotel, 50 years old, naked, one hand raised, another on a hip,
poised like a flamingo dancing, a solemn face under bright lights.
"Make love to me, please." Make love to me, Robert called.
4am brought a brighter shining light, dawn
arrived in 1979. The year you were born.
Fast forward: Robert's son's grown up, becomes a hippie, died.
Robert married, divorced, remarried,
he locked away his Leica, took up filmmaking then only shot Polaroids,
"Polaroid—passed quickly,
images fade gradually—like a life opposed to preservation,"
you wrote in your notes on Robert Frank,
how his later photos made you burst into tears,
separation, love, so many separations, you experienced it all.
We eventually married, you continued writing poetry, fairy tales,
taking photos with a pinhole camera, consumed by countless new projects;
you ran away from home, climbed over the wall of a student hostel and fled,
          losing your way in Beijing and Guangzhou,

你的身體接納過愛你的人也接納過陌生人，
鏡頭去到今夜，你又乘坐夜機北上，在星海中浮沉。
"凌晨4點，和我做愛"，這時候我翻過羅伯特
《我的掌紋》攝影集，便不可抑制地想你。
想抱緊你在萬里高空中一具有血有肉的身體，
一起走進過去的、未來的、迎面而來的萬頃空虛，
走進我們毫不懼怕的死。說：
"凌晨4點，和我做愛"。

your body taking in people who loved you and also strangers,
the camera pans to tonight, you're on an evening flight north, drifting in
                    a sea of stars.
"4am, make love to me," as I'm skimming Robert's filmography
*The Lines of My Hand*, I can't not miss you thousands of miles up in the sky.
I think of holding you tight, your flesh and blood,
walking together into a thousand-hectare void of the past, of the future,
                    of the next moment,
walking into death, of which we've never been afraid. Saying
"4am, make love to me."

# 查理穿過廟街
## ——或：我們是不是的士司機？

在阿高家重看了三十年前的反叛電影
《的士司機》。就著血腥和憤怒
喝啤酒。過時的純潔使我們的欲望變得懷舊，
查理建議我和他到廟街，撇下被愛情光顧的阿高。

這個議題其實早就是我一首詩的預備題目，
但我想寫的是《查理穿過鴨寮街》，我想寫
他拿起滿街的舊相機、舊唱片時的快樂，還有
那些賣舊貨的老頭們的快樂。我想寫，我們未老先衰。

廟街也是一個好題材，那裡新東西的殘舊
不亞於鴨寮街舊東西的新奇。
查理，和我一樣出生於七十年代，卻鍾情於更早的
六十年代。他甚至跟五十年代也能融為一體：

走到哪裡，他就是哪裡的奇蹟。滿街
廉價貨湧向我們，琳琅滿目的野史、冒險紀和情慾。
《的士司機》的饑餓得由玩具汽車和玩具槍來餵飽，
我們穿過那些鍍金的日子，彷彿兩個視察農村的領導。

只有不歇的掌聲提醒我們注意別的演員，
我們是在錢幣的喧嘩中謝幕的失業漢。
他一年沒畫一幅畫，只有我還稱他為畫家，
我指點他觀看地攤上層層疊疊的梵．高的翻版。

# Charlie on Temple Street
### —or: are we the Taxi Driver?

At Ar Kao's place we watch the thirty-year-old cult classic
*Taxi Driver*. Our blood and anger mix
with beer. Its dated innocence turns our desire to nostalgia.
Charlie suggests heading down to Temple Street, leaving love-struck
                      Ar Kao behind.

I was considering "Charlie Walks Down Apliu Street" for a poem,
I wanted to write about the joy of picking up old cameras, vinyl,
aging shopkeepers selling secondhand goods,
I wanted to write about growing old in our youth.

But Temple Street's a good subject too, the antiquated look of new things
compared to the newness of old things on Apliu Street.
Charlie and I were both born in the '70s, in love with the late
'60s, occasionally communing with the '50s:

He uncovers the miracle of each place. Low-priced goods
spill out on the street—a dazzling unofficial history, adventure story, desire.
The Taxi Driver's hunger is fed by toy cars and guns.
We pass through gilded days like a couple of village inspectors.

Only the nonstop applause reminds us there are other actors.
we are shiftless, responding to curtain calls, the clamor of coins.
He hasn't painted in a year but I still call him a painter,
I point out the numerous van Gogh copies scattered over the ground.

"勇氣畢竟可嘉！"我如此贊歎，
"你還要注意到它們都用了大刀闊斧的油彩。"
其實我還是想為自己尋找安慰。一個個尼泊爾女人
貢獻著對麻織品的崇拜；一個個算命先生詛咒我們去死！

他們溫厚的臉，他們英勇的眉毛又騙倒了
多少沉醉於厄運的青年。啤酒的麻醉還沒消除，
厄運又來纏繞我們的腳：你的腳，牛仔褲綻開了線頭；
你的鞋多麼骯髒——我的血也不遑多讓。

查理的目光只為舊社會所吸引，
但賣家們敲打瓷器或者表蓋就能聽出
我們空蕩的回聲。我翻動一件件夏威夷襯衫和異國情侶
——我迫不及待奔向切．格瓦拉的紅色鬍鬚！

還是《的士司機》的問題，我們疼痛的手掌
無法把手槍抓得更緊！"你忍心向這些擁有厄運者開槍嗎？
你忍心不和他們一起分享厄運嗎？"我的後褲兜裡
還放著幾塊嶄新的硬幣。

不，查理，他的台詞應該是這樣："我要贖回
這個世界血淋淋的象徵嗎？我要贖回
這些面具、禮服、假皮鞋和翻唱CD嗎？"我
把一大袋書從左手換到右手，我把思路的死胡同換來換去。

我們沿著廟街一直往前，走到盡頭折回來
我才知道我們不是在兜圈子。也不是兜售
自己破舊的記憶。算命先生們，祖國觀光客們
遍地的文物應該回歸，遍地的安迪．沃霍爾應該升天！

"It's a form of courage," I praise,
"See, how wildly and ferociously they paint."
I'd still like to find a way to comfort myself. A Nepalese woman
worshipping linens; a fortune-teller announcing our impending dooms!

Their gentle faces display a kindness, their brave eyebrows deceive
youth captivated by misfortune. Still numb from the beer,
misfortune slaps us: frayed jeans on your legs;
your worn and dirty shoes—my blood's the same.

Charlie's eyes are trapped in the old world,
by tapping the porcelain and watch covers, vendors can distinguish
our hollow echo. I come upon a Hawaiian shirt with foreign lovers
—rush hastily to Che Guevara's red beards!

Again, we return to the question of the Taxi Driver, our aching palms
can't grasp the gun tighter! "Are you cruel enough to gun down the owner
                    of all these misfortunes?
Are you heartless enough not to share their misfortunes?" A few brand-new
                    coins in my back pocket.

No, Charlie, the lines should be: "Should I redeem
the bloody signs of this world?" Should I buy back
those masks, cocktail dresses, fake leather shoes and pirated CDs? I
switch the bag of books to my right hand, my train of thought ending
                    in one alley after the next.

We walk down Temple Street, to the end and turn back
to make sure we're not going in circles, not selling off
our worn memories. Listen, fortune-tellers, visitors from the motherland,
all these strewn antiques should be returned, Andy Warhols should ascend
                    to the heavens!

唉，我重看三十年前的朋克司機才知道有一個
妓女一家大團圓的結局。我三十年的憤怒形同虛設，
對著滿世界心滿意足的殺手們我的血無處發洩。
但查理表示對導演的理解：他可不是查理．卓別林。

難道我們只能思考廟街的佈景、光線？
怎麼剪接我斷落的肋骨？你
等待付款的青春片場？查理明天能挖到他的金礦嗎？
我明天能發行我盜版香港的悲劇嗎？能不能

回到廟街的入口來。兩台戲此起彼伏叫囂，
老花旦、老樂手們拉扯著六十七年前的琴弦、鼓鈸，
把我們的記憶撕碎。最後只剩下魚蛋檔的老闆在憤怒，
他憤怒地微笑，嘿！我們就找他來當替身。

查理，保留你的鬍子吧，它們揭示了你的真實年歲。
最後，讓我們回到廟街的入口來，
在血泊中把手槍藏好。在血泊中有華麗的浪潮，
讓我們走。最後，讓我們回到廟街的入口來。

Watching the punk driver thirty years later I discover
it all ends happily for the hooker. My thirty years of anger were in vain,
facing a world of perfectly content killers, my blood has nowhere to go,
but Charlie empathizes with the director: hey, at least he isn't Chaplin.

Is it impossible for us to think past the lights and setting of Temple Street?
Edit out my broken ribs? You
standing in line for a kid's film? Will Charlie unearth some gold tomorrow?
Will I release my pirated Hong Kong tragedy? Will I

head back to the start of Temple Street. Two competing stages—
old huadans, musicians plucking tunes from the '60s, strings and cymbals,
shredding our memories, dashing from the rage of a fish-ball stand owner,
smiling in anger! Hey, let's pull him in as an extra.

Charlie, keep your beard, it shows your true age.
Let's go back to the start of Temple Street,
conceal the gun in blood. A splendid wave of blood,
come on. Let's go back to the start of Temple Street.

# 皇后碼頭歌謠

共你淒風苦雨
共你披星戴月
　　　——周耀輝《皇后大盜》

那夜我看見一垂釣者把一根白燭
放進碼頭前深水，給鬼魂們引路。
嗚嗚，我是一陣風，在此縈繞不肯去。

那夜我看見一弈棋者把棋盤填字，
似是九龍墨跡家譜零碎然而字字天書。
嗚嗚，我是一陣風，在此縈繞不肯去。

那夜我看見一舞者把一襲白裙
舞成流云，云上有金猴怒目切齒。
吁吁，我是一陣雨，在此淅瀝不肯去。

那夜我看見一喪妻者敲盆而歌，
歌聲清越仿如四十年前一少年無忌。
吁吁，我是一陣雨，在此淅瀝不肯去。

"共你披星戴月……"今夜我在碼頭燒信，
群魔在都市的千座針尖上升騰，
我共你煮雨焚風，喚一場熔爐中的飛霜。

咄咄，我是一個人，在此咬指、書空。

# The Ballad of Queen's Pier

*With you through bleak wind and wretched rain*
*With you cloaked by the moon, capped in stars*
——Chow Yiu Fai "Queen's Robber"

That night I watched a fisherman place a white candle
in the water along the pier, leading the way for ghosts.
Whoosh, I was a gust of wind, lingering, unwilling to leave.

That night I watched a chess-player filling words on the chessboard,
piecemeal as a genealogy in Kowloon ink, each word as mystical.
Whoosh, I was a gust of wind, lingering, unwilling to leave.

That night I watched a dancer whirl a white dress
into flowing clouds, upon the clouds a golden monkey gnashed his teeth
                with fierce eyes.
Shu shu, I was a shower, pattering away, unwilling to leave.

That night I watched a widower drum on a pan and sing,
a song as clear and strong as a fearless youth of forty years ago.
Shu shu, I was a shower, pattering away, unwilling to leave.

"With you cloaked by the moon, capped in stars." Tonight I burn
                letters at the pier,
demons rise up on the city's thousand needles,
with you I boil rain and burn wind, call for sleet in a melting pot.

Tut tut, I am human, bite my finger, write in the sky.

# 香港島未來史

5000年後，水位線
還好只上升到了德輔道、莊士敦道，
海水獺和老鼠在半淹的會展新翼骨架上
做了幾百個窩，在國際金融中心
做了上千個。雨不停下著
一把傘在一堆立法會的亂石中出土。
電車軌上的鏽有一寸厚，
誰在做夢聽到叮噹叮噹？
彈塗魚把北角和西營盤佔領，
那裏的老街道輕易還原成泥，
它們也有了更強壯的肺。
它們不好吃而且其大如豬，
像獵人而不是獵物
甚至有厚甲充當盾牌。
人大概還有幾百個，孤獨
散居在銅鑼灣、金鐘和中環的廢墟，
每人假裝擁有一朵雲
裏面有足以淹死其他所有人的雨水，
但他們吃的，是一種特殊的蟲子
它能夠消化電子板和光纖
是祖先留下來的寶貴財富。
這些人還在東躲西藏
因為來自黃竹坑的巨貓意外地
繁殖反常，佔領了大半個香港。

10000年後，雨停了
你仍能在海上辨認出這小島，
冰塊碰撞著，寫下不文明的花紋，

24

# The Future History of Hong Kong Island

5,000 years from now the water line
will rise to Des Voeux and Johnston Roads,
sea otters and rats will make hundreds of holes in the frame of
the half-flooded new wing of the HKCEC, more than a thousand holes
in the IFC. The rain will be constant.
An umbrella will be unearthed in the rubble of the Legislative Council.
There will be an inch of rust on the tram tracks.
Who will dream and hear the ding-ding ding-ding?
Mudskippers will occupy North Point and Sai Ying Pun,
old streets will again become mud,
they will have stronger lungs.
they will not be as delicious or as large as a pig,
like hunters but not hunted.
they will even have carapaces for shields,
there will be hundreds of people, lonely,
scattered in ruins in Causeway Bay, Admiralty and Central.
Everyone will pretend to own a cloud
of rain water that can drown everything else,
they will eat a special worm
which can digest electronic boards and optical fibers,
a precious heritage left behind by ancestors.
These people will be in hiding and dodging
because the pandas in Wong Chuk Hang have reproduced
abnormally and occupy most of Hong Kong.

19,000 years from now, the rain will have stopped,
you still will be able to recognize this tiny island in the sea,
blocks of ice will clash, and write uncivilized patterns,

巨大的冰窟偶爾呈現出原來的形狀：
10000年前的圓盤、方塊和塔尖，
誰在做夢聽到叮噹叮噹？
長毛鼠群據於此，尚未發明出文字，
頻密的閃電烤熟了其中數十隻
釋放出吸引陸鯊的香氣。
陸鯊只能在沒有結冰的地方登陸
例如跑馬地和柴灣
一些十字架和碑石提供攀爬的方便，
它們蹣跚著好像人類的嬰兒，
哀哀的叫聲也像人類的嬰兒，
看到這一幕會令你落淚
假如你在北極
安達露米星人的集中營逃了出來。
要是這樣請你逃到摩星嶺去
那裏又長出了不畏嚴寒的苔蘚
能讓你果腹，保有精力
去迎接下一個千年的酷熱或洪水。

100000年後，它終於不是島
成為大陸塊的一個小尖疣
蠅飛魚們在這裏呼聚
它們朝生暮死，因為瘋狂的天氣，
它們希望自己有一個靈魂，
有一個囚禁新貴的捕魚猴的地獄。
海水已經不可能帶走這裏的一絲東西
一種綿延數百公里的藤蔓
把薄扶林、香港仔和石澳緊緊裹住。
誰在做夢聽到叮噹叮噹？
99900年前人類挖掘的地下城
終於被藤蔓的根全部佔據

some of the discs, blocks and spires maintain their original shape:
A circle from 10,000 years ago.
Who will dream and hear the ding-ding ding-ding?
Long-haired hamsters will gather but haven't yet invented words,
the frequent lightning will cook dozens of them,
emitting a smell that attracts land sharks.
Land sharks can only come ashore at places without ice
like Happy Valley and Chai Wan.
Some crosses and monuments will be easy to climb,
they will walk haltingly like human babies,
they will cry like human babies, too,
you will weep when you see this, just like
you'd escaped from the Andalumi aliens
concentration camp at the North Pole.
If so, please escape to Mount Davis
where moss and lichen grow that withstands bitter cold,
that will let you fill your belly to conserve your strength,
to be ready for the heat waves or floods in the next millennium.


A 100,000 years from now, it will no longer be an island
but a small wart on a large continent,
fly-flying-fishes will gather here,
born at dawn and dead at dusk with the chaotic weather,
they hope for a soul
and a hell to imprison the upstart fish-hunting monkeys.
It is no longer possible for the sea to wash anything away,
a several-hundred-kilometer vine
will have tightly bound Pokfulam, Aberdeen and Shek O.
Who will dream and hear the ding-ding ding-ding?
The underground city dug by human beings 99,900 years before
finally will have been occupied by the vine's roots.

他們為迎接世界末日屯積的
豐富的鐵和石油
竟然成了藤蔓繁衍的堆肥。
全球化在真正意義來臨了，
香港仍然是地球上唯一大陸的
先進一隅。

Abundant iron and oil
accumulated for the end of the world
becomes unintentional fertilizer for propagating the vine.
Globalization truly will have arrived,
Hong Kong will remain an advanced corner of the earth's
sole continent.

# 在北京看香港七一遊行紀錄片

我好像是焦裂的皇后大道
被他們反對和踐踏，因我不在，
我應該在灣仔停駛的電車旁邊，
看見自己被同樣的厲火燃點。

但我竟已被另一個城市軟禁，
每天任它用甜言蜜語占建。
這裏夏天的枝葉在恐怖過後
過分地茂盛，把雷雨強行遮掩。

我一遍遍重看那短短的錄影
頭腦中也喧騰、萬人空巷，
我推開窗，張開嘴，
這嘴巴馬上被新世界的瓦礫填滿。

我看見三年前的我振臂，無聲，
如訊號的剎那中斷，旋即無形。
我欣喜於他額上仍有汗，臉上有怒，
唇邊有微笑，即使無字寫出。

我被那只越過虛無伸出的手接上，
猛然發現自己回到了炎夏之海。
毒辣的陽光刈割我的脊背
一如刈割眾生的脊背。

# In Beijing, I Watch a Documentary
## of the July 1 Hong Kong March

I am like the burning, crackling Queen's Road
opposed to and trampled on, because I'm not there,
I should have been in Wan Chai, next to the halted tram,
watching myself ignite in the same flame.

But I've been detained by another city,
each day letting myself grow possessed by its sweet words.
Hereafter the terror, branches and leaves
flourishing all summer, provide shelter against thunder and rain.

I play the recording over and over,
my mind roiling, the entire city turns out,
I open the windows, and my mouth
immediately fills up with debris from the new world.

I see myself three years before, raising my arm, voiceless,
as if the signal has been promptly disconnected, instantly growing formless.
I'm delighted there's still sweat on his forehead, anger on his face,
a smile on his mouth, though not a single word can be written down.

I've been caught by an outstretched hand which bridges the void,
abruptly discovering I've gone back to the sea of a burning summer.
Furious sunlight slashes cruelly across my back
like it cuts the back of all living things.

鐵應該摧毀鐵，如像長江。
不必要的詩歌應該噤聲。
我聽說：一個人正在消失的涪陵死去；
與此同時，洪水已經淹沒了鐵路沿線。

Iron should destroy iron, like the Yangtze.
Unnecessary poems should keep their mouths shut.
I've heard someone is dying in vanishing Fuling;
floods have submerged all the rail lines.

# 寫完一首反戰詩走出家門

寫完一首反戰詩走出家門，
正午，陽光彷彿巨輪停泊，然而乘客全無。
雲團彷彿兵團——停泊鳳凰山、陰雨山上。

這是七月的怨靈，本應在地中海邊上
咀嚼微甜草根的；現在和陽光糾纏著
來到我被炸開的天空。

寂靜密集爆破，耳膜和蟋蟀同時感到
它們輕輕一跳便是天國。
死者何在？我剛寫完一首挽歌。

我出門迎接的既是我的新娘也是彈雨；
我們中午喝的既是喜酒也是苦艾；
我們穿過的既是東涌也是逃往塞浦路斯的路，

我們和異族的鬼做愛，彷彿伊凡在照明彈下渡河，
在冰冷的水汽中摸著了亡友的骨骼，
這是他的手指他的手肘他星光四散的頭顱。

## "After writing an anti-war poem I leave the house"

After writing an anti-war poem I leave the house,
noon, sunlight anchored like an ocean liner with no passengers,
clouds anchored like a military detachment on Lantau Peak, overcast, rain.

A vengeful July spirit once found on Mediterranean shores
chews sweet stalks of grass; tangled in sunlight,
comes to my shattered sky.

An intense burst of silence felt by eardrums and crickets,
for whom gently hopping is the kingdom of heaven.
Where are the dead? I've just finished an elegy.

I leave the house, meeting my bride in a hail of bullets;
our wedding banquet's at noon to be accompanied with absinthe;
passing through Tung Chung, escaping along the road to Cyprus,

We make love with a ghost from a foreign tribe, like Ivan crossing a river
                    beneath a flare,
caressing the bones of our dead friend in a freezing mist,
this his finger, an elbow, his light-diffused skull.

# 霧 · 太平山頂

我們像兒童麥兜，興沖沖鑽進
無翅纜車，駛進蓬草長葉覆蓋的山中，
枝葉尚未伸進我們的衣袖，
突然山頂大霧撲將下來，迅速淹過

我們，像負資產把中年麥兜沒頂。
山頂上，醉倒的太平，大霧中九一一屬於
你們——在消防燈中奔跑的蠟像人，
急速送我們扭曲的酒瓶、老年的望遠鏡。

山徑中，樹分着濃淡，不再走出
搖鈴人。今天，我是我自己的老襯
將到伶仃洋中蓋一座亭，"亭中有奇樹……"

我可以攀、可以嘉其聲、可以哭其燦爛。
山的輪廓搖曳着，向大海移動：
我可以抹去萬戶，只憑冤魂麥兜，天蓬一閃。

# Fog: Taiping Shan Peak

We are like a young McDull, happily cramming
onto a wingless tram, driving into a mountain wrapped in weeds and leaves,
leaves and branches not yet stretched in our sleeves
as the peak fog swoops, flooding across.

We are like negative equity sinking a middle-aged McDull.
Drunken Taiping peak, 9/11 in the fog belongs
to you—wax figures dashing under the light of a fire brigade,
hastily delivering us contorted wine bottles, telescopes for old age.

Along the mountain trail trees run thick and thin, but the bell ringer
never appears. Today I am my own idiot lover
heading to the Lingding Sea to build a pavilion,
          "In the pavilion there is a strange tree . . ."

I can climb it, praise its fame, weep at its brilliance.
The mountain's flickering silhouette moves towards the sea:
I can obliterate thousands of homes with just McDull's repressed soul,
          the twinkling of Tianpeng.

# 讀新興縣誌

瘴癘地變魍魎者千萬，我是其外萬一
荔枝花沖天香陣，我是其外萬一

年複年大旱、大澇，甚至雹大如拳
風雪、怪獸和逐臣也輪番光顧這一小縣

我是其外萬一，出生入死，有口難言
的一個獦獠，猶負水、伐竹、射鹿、深耕

最後全化爲烏有，如民初時一場場大火
我傾盡護城池水也不能救

何況我滴水未傾。我只是挾鳥槍上山
化身猛虎吹笛，吹滿天彩雲

我就在這天地遺忘了的一隅食粽
粽子裏包裹一把最綠的綠豆

荔枝是年又大豐收，林蔭漫到了鄰村
寂靜是天堂給我的一紙赦令

# Reading the Xinxing County Gazetteer

Millions transformed into demons in a malaria-ridden land, I was one
               of the millions
the scent of lychee flowers transcending heaven, I was one of the millions

Year after year of drought, floods and hailstones as large as fists
snowstorms, monsters and exiled officers take turns visiting the small county

I was one of the millions, risking my life, with an ineffable toughness
a Geliao, still carrying water, cutting bamboo, hunting deer, farming

Everything eventually vanished, like the huge fires of Republican times
which were never extinguished even with the county's entire water supply

Needless to say, I never use them. I take only a musket into the mountains
transformed into a fierce tiger, playing the flute, blowing colorful clouds
               into the sky

That day I left behind a rice dumpling
wrapped around a handful of the greenest green beans

This year will be another plentiful lychee harvest, leaves casting shade
               across neighboring villages,
silence is a pardon heaven decrees to me

# 最好的時光

現世糟糕，我飛離寒冷的香港，
飛過炎熾的台北、脂粉暖人的北京，
在飛機越過東京的淫雨之後，
白令海峽終於圍抱著我。它沒有定語，

彷彿安慰。飛機及時播出《最好的時光》，
侯孝賢傷心，傷心得一塌糊塗，
精心選擇的悲歌縈繞我剩下的旅途，
那音樂一再沉落、一再委婉，
那男孩傾訴如我年輕時絕望，絕望但馥鬱。

沉重的鮮花開滿那些孤寂時光，
我嘆飲那流金的夜露，兀自書寫
花葉點綴輕若無物的朝雲。

這是最好的也是最壞的時光，
我仿若狄更斯的幽靈遊蕩在北美大陸，
在安大略湖邊，托著頭好象一個印第安人
托著死鷹的羽骨。

多倫多陰晴變幻，我在黑暗中
嘗試抄下去國的梁啟超寫於馬關之詩、
廖偉棠寫於北京之詩，皆嶄新如雪，
黑暗裏入舒琪薄旗袍，裏入我

歸程如餓鬼道。回來的飛機壞了，
我不能再看一遍《最好的時光》，
只知道白令海峽遠遠鋪展，左右伸開雙手：
亞洲和美洲，它豁達依舊、一如絕望依舊。

# The Best of Times

The world today is a mess. I fly from the cold of Hong Kong,
over blazing Taipei, rouged and warm Beijing,
soaring over Tokyo's heavy rains,
the Bering Strait finally embracing me. It's featurelessness

is comforting. *The Best of Times* starts at precisely the right moment,
Hou Hsiao-Hsien is so unhappy he's completely baffled,
a carefully chosen sad song affects me the rest of the journey,
music descending again and again, euphemizing again and again,
boy's pouring out the despair of my youth, despairing and fragrant.

Heavy flowers blossoming at a lonely time,
I sip evening's golden dew, still writing
the weightless cloud of dawn embellished in flowers and leaves.

This is the best of times, this is the worst of times.
I wander North America like the ghost of Charles Dickens
on the banks of Lake Ontario, I raise my head like an Indian
holding the feathers and bones of a dead eagle.

Toronto could be overcast or fine, I'm in the dark
attempting to copy "Shimonoseki" by Liang Qichao, the diaspora,
a poem written by Liu Waitong in Beijing, both like brand-new snow,
darkness wrapped within me in Shu Qi's shear qipao.

The return flight is just like the Preta realm. The monitor is broken,
so I can't watch *The Best of the Times* again,
knowing the Bering Strait sprawls below, stretching its arms left and right:
Asia and America, sanguine as always, despairing as always.

## 有人在火焰裏捉迷藏

有人在黑暗中求光明；
有人擎花走，走進尼姑庵；
有人昨夜渡輪上，看驟雨海面上升騰；
有人轉工轉車，頻頻更換證件相；
有人把舊銅像磨出了光；
有人掀起一段鐵路尋找一粒草芥；
有人在紅布包上畫臉，星星點點；
有人深呼吸，被大霧淹斃；
有人傾囊而出，放煙花叢叢；
有人乘興遊山從此不見；
有人垂釣，因爲一個夢而升官；
有人赤條條來去，大雪落滿身；
有人捕獲了雷公打算作爲佳肴；
有人興建了樂園，表演舔刀刃；
有人下煤窯四個月，得小說一篇；
有人要在臨汾興建天安門；
有人甘掏五萬與施瓦辛格進餐；
有人爲藝術隆胸並拒絕富商出價五百萬；
有人戴黑紗到政府總部上班；
有人把自己當飛機把蝴蝶結當螺旋槳；
有人摸黑掄斧，不惜自傷；
有人畫闖銀行，得鏽鏡一枚；
有人恩愛後翻臉，出示警官證；
有人瞎眼攀上通天藤；
有人在暴雨中酌酒獨飲；
有人辭官歸故里；
有人漏夜趕科場；

# Someone Plays Hide-and-Seek in the Flame

Someone seeks brightness in the dark;
Someone holds flowers, walking into a nunnery;
Someone watches a rain storm rising from the harbor, last night's ferry;
Someone changes cars frequently, jobs and passport photos;
Someone scours aging bronze statues until they shine;
Someone raises up the whole rail in order to dust;
Someone, in bits and pieces, draws faces on red bags;
Someone breathes in deeply, is drowned by the fog;
Someone empties their wallet to field a grove of fireworks;
Someone merrily sets off hiking and is never seen again;
Someone fishes, gets promoted through a dream;
Someone comes and goes in the nude, covered in snow;
Someone catches the God of Thunder with plans to turn him into a great dish;
Someone builds an amusement park and licks the edge of a sword;
Someone goes into a coal mine for four months and finishes a novel;
Someone wants to build a Tiananmen in Linfen;
Someone is willing to pay fifty thousand for a meal with Schwarzenegger;
Someone gets breast implants for art's sake and refuses a tycoon's five million;
Someone wears black armbands and works at government headquarters;
Someone is convinced they're a plane with a bow for a propeller;
Someone brandishes an axe in the dark, potentially injuring themselves;
Someone rushes into a bank at noon and steals a rusty mirror;
Someone breaks up after a fling and then flashes a police badge;
Someone climbs a towering beanstalk blind;
Someone sips wine alone in a rainstorm;
Someone resigns and returns to their hometown;
Someone rushes to an examination hall at night;

有人，在火焰裏捉迷藏，
全都，在火焰裏捉迷藏，
一個兵、一個賊，一個賊、一個兵……
夢裏不知風吹血，醒來方覺梟噬心。

Someone plays hide-and-seek in the flame;
Everyone plays hide-and-seek in the flame;
A soldier, a thief, a thief, a soldier . . .
In the dream the wind felt like it was pelting my blood. Awake,
an owl was gnawing at my heart.

# 春天的現實主義勞動者

想起來好象是多么遙遠的事，
整個春天我們都在黑暗的田野上揮動
捕蝶網，在黑暗的風中。黑暗一縷縷
流過網眼，雖然濃稠但還是落空。
夜深時我們遇見那個人稱"蜻蜓老"的老人，
他給我們講了許多故事：關於
製造月亮的工廠的故事，關於遠古
小兄妹亂倫的故事，還有少年變成怪魚的故事。
我們打了一個又一個呵欠，在寒意中一躍而起，
一下子饑餓如同夜鷹，巨網在空中攪動出星星。
嗨喲，汗水刺骨意味著快樂，而風愈暖。
嗨喲，公路被掀起了，祖國有了花邊，
在我們所不知道的世界，朝野起了嘩變，
新聞受到控制，炮彈在炮腔中卡住爆炸了。
我們做著夢然後被夢絆倒：夢裏有墳。
我們索性坐下來向墳中垂釣，
鬼於是出來，"沽酒來乎？少年！"
是亦非哉天老矣！躅髏爲杯非今世也！

# Realist Laborer in Spring

When I think about it now, it seems so long ago,
waving butterfly nets all spring
in a dark field, in a dark wind. Darkening wisps
flew through the net; though a thick mesh we always missed.
At night we met the old man known as "Mr. Dragonfly."
He told us endless stories:
about a moon-manufacturing factory, about incest
between siblings in ancient times, a young man becoming a strange fish.
Yawn after yawn, in the cold we jumped up,
we grew as hungry as nighthawks, the huge net stirred stars in the sky.
Yo-ho! Bone-chilling sweat means happiness, and the wind grows warmer.
Yo-ho! The road rises and the motherland is laced by a new border.
We had no sense of the wider world, that there'd been a coup;
news was controlled, cannon balls jammed then exploded in the barrel.
We were dreaming and tripped: there was a grave in the dream.
We simply sat down and dropped a hook into the grave,
then a ghost appears, "Brought you some wine, young man?"
Hasn't heaven grown old? Skeletons no longer used for cups of wine!

# 在和平時期

我們流亡在和平時期，對外稱
是一場場即興的旅遊，對內是戰火處處
焚燒我們隨身攜帶的一片深秀。

儘管百姓鏖戰於商業、逸樂，且地產商
一再把他們的山水更新出桃源的血泊，
我們仍追隨了濃墨偏鋒的一筆——

七十年前奧登在中國丟失了衣修午德，
即使他們都學得了古中國人
眸子的清澈。今天，我們丟失了中國。

2.
丟失就是認識。在戰時，哀歌
等於愛歌，我們在嬰孩的哭聲中
離開這座城市，趕去溺愛另一座痛哭的城市。

猶如一個巨嬰，艱難轉頭看另一個巨嬰
——他正在產床的中心擊掌，他似笑
尚未大笑，亂發脾氣的時刻還未來臨。

但他已經懂得把RMB換成USD，
把美麗定義爲美利堅。愛歌換爲哀歌，
是我們對他唯一的打算。

# In Time of Peace

We head into exile in time of peace, claiming to the outside
world it's spontaneous travel. To the inner self it's all out war
burning an elegance carried within.

People are at odds over commerce and pleasure, while developers
keep turning mountains and rivers into Shangri-las filled with blood,
we keep following the dark colors and slanting strokes—

Seventy years ago Auden lost Isherwood in China,
even though they'd learned the distinct precepts
of ancient China. Today, we have lost China.


2.

Losing by knowing. In time of war, a mourning song
is a love song. Amidst the sound of crying babies, we
leave this city and rush to spoil another wailing city.

Like a giant baby craning its neck to look at another giant baby
—he is clapping hands in the middle of the bed, appearing to smile,
but not laughing. The tantrum is yet to come.

He already knows how to convert RMB to USD,
and America is defined as Amazing. Our only plan for him
is to turn love songs into songs of mourning.

### 3.

山水酣暢，出落一派悲觀；
人民酣暢，嘔吐各自混沌的畫中天。
在哈爾濱，我們丟失了東北烈士紀念館。

正如我們在洞庭丟失了天下之憂。
在鳳凰丟失了苗人蠱，在平遙丟失了
烽火台。在難民中卻發現了徐霞客。

而不是徐霞村、戴望舒與施蟄存，
二十年代迅速跑出赤色，猶抹血迷眼；
二十世紀迅速跑進黑色，猶能鍍金。

### 4.

寒山碧水有奪命金，
黑山白水又如何？
祖國遽然對我們變臉。

你在光前揮手，帶出熠熠
是我們的旅程，露天電影燒著空白
的一段膠片，黑山白水，又豈不是黑水白山？

祖國呵，我在胸中細理那栩栩柳煙，
那都是你扔棄給我的，那都是我藉以
偷渡戰火的盤川。

3.

Carefree landscapes give birth to pessimism;
Carefree people vomit chaotic skies onto paintings.
In Harbin, we've lost the Northeast Martyrs Memorial Hall.

Just as we've lost all concern for the world in Dongting Lake,
we've lost Miao black magic in Fenghuang, and the beacon tower
in Pingyao. We've discovered Xu Xiake among the refugees.

But not Xu Xiacun, Dai Wangshu or Shi Zhecun,
in the 1920s red ran out quickly, but blood still blurs the eyes;
in the 20th century, black ran in quickly, but still grows gold plated.


4.

There are perilous golds in cold mountains and blue rivers,
so what about black mountains and white rivers?
The motherland abruptly turns hostile.

You wave hands in front of the light, our journey
is that bright. The outdoor movie is burning
empty films. Are black mountains and white rivers only black mountains
                    and white rivers?

Oh Motherland, in my mind I take care of the vivid smoke,
which is all you've thrown at me, which is what I used to pay
for my travel expenses to escape the flames of war.

### 5.

從東三省下到北平，人民怒而不爭，
從關外回到北京，人民的甲兵
一致向內。宣傳移動著邊界

修訂著規矩：酒肉換作了榮辱
仍然與酒肉同義；擊柝者搜集民謠
竟相當於與虎謀皮。

在北京桃花仍然蒙塵，夜行之，畫伏之，
最後一個暗殺家找不到菜市口，
在美術館剖腹，爲無名山再增高一米。

### 6.

資本也自詡過自己的非俗之美，
我們見到他演出，從街頭到電視，
他聲嘶力竭帶領全國翻新：

在北京他如水蛋體育館般可愛，
在上海他是一個老賭徒僞裝了新手，
並隨時準備獻出自己陳舊的私處。

而事實是動物園門前豎立了京巴狗
足以令萬獸噤聲，既然狗要吠叫
人民要合照，我們何必絕食，咆哮？

5.

From three Northeast Provinces to Peiping, people are angry but not fighting
from regions outside the Pass to Beijing, the people's army
turns their guns inward. Propaganda moves the boundary

and amends the rule: wine and meat are substitutes for glory and humiliation
but the meaning is the same; when the guard collects folk songs
he is asking a tiger for its skin.

In Beijing, peach blossoms remain in exile, fleeing at night, hiding at dawn,
the last assassin cannot locate the Beijing food market;
so he takes his own life in the art museum, adding one more meter to the
anonymous mountain.


6.

Capital has praised its otherworldly beauty,
we can see his performance from the streets to the TV,
shouting loudly to lead the country's renewal:

in Beijing he's as cute as the egg-like stadium,
in Shanghai he's an experienced gambler pretending to be a novice,
ready to donate his aging private parts.

In fact, a Pekingese lion-dog statue erected in front of the zoo
is enough to silence thousands of animals. When dogs want to bark
and people take photos, why must we go on hunger strike and roar?

### 7.

來自陝西的灰北京中午吃清晨吃，
結果卻吃得越來越象一個江南胖子，
只有西山依舊，山陰仍擁翠微。

溪水漲，載酒可以行，
韓博不是韓愈，虛無猶迎佛骨？
高曉濤也不是高適，刀劍殺出羅漢？

王煒離開王維，假裝戍邊。我離開北京
假裝擁有李賀的夜色，轉瞬間晞薄——
來自渤海的日出我們黑夜裏吃。

### 8.

國富山河在，歌舞幾時休？
腰纏百萬貫的人過了揚州到杭州
正好煮累死的鶴，而我們索性幫他拆琴。

焚琴的木炭從江南一路扔至嶺南，
一路鏗鏘有聲。今天，美景需要塗鴉手，
古琴只是量販KTV裏的幫兇。

而我們需要更黑的顏料畫城市的真容，
首先如木刻刀剜出1910年的滬杭線！
接著洗筆，如洗秋瑾血，把西湖洗成墨池。

7.

Grey Beijing from Shaanxi eats at noon, he eats at dawn,
and starts to look like a fatty from Jiangnan,
only Xishan remains the same and Shanyin stays green.

The stream rises and holds wine,
Han Bo is not Han Yu. Can nothingness welcome the bone of the Buddha?
Gao Xiaotao is also not Gao Shi. Will arhats flee between swords?

Wang Wei leaves Wang Wei, pretending to defend the border. I leave Beijing
pretending to take hold of Li He's night scene, which quickly wears thin—
the sun rises in Bohai, we eat at night.

8.

The country's rich and mountains and rivers remain, when will the singing
                and dancing end?
The man with millions in cash strung to his belt left Yangzhou for Hangzhou,
he cooks an exhausted crane, we help him break a qin.

Charcoal which burns the qin is tossed from Jiangnan to Lingnan,
rhythmic and sonorous. Nowadays, a beautiful scene requires graffitists,
ancient qins are nothing more than accomplices in karaoke boxes.

And we need a darker black ink to draw the real city.
First, carve the 1910 Shanghai-Hangzhou Railway with a woodcutting knife!
Next, wash the brush like washing the blood of Qiu Jin and turn West Lake
                into a pool of ink.

9.

悲傷的是山水抬升了地價，還兀自秀麗，
黃賓虹的叛軍已經被逐出國外，
悲傷的是雲還路過中國，江南自晴雨。

幸存者無傘，暴雨裏過蘇、白堤，
四十年前的冤獄被洗得一乾二淨，
我舉起相機拍攝他，只拍得白茫茫

一圈水汽。他驚惶地揮手拒絕——
"別拍我，這二千年的佈景更美！"
要是美是幫兇，我索性上桃花島，入瓦崗寨！


10.

是的不可能再美了，山河竟然
未毀，但同時我們胸有草木深，
掄斧斤向此金明，血泊變鳴禽。

四十年前這裏有無名氏，死於無何有之國，
仍如張志新，仍如劉和珍、徐錫麟，
一百年前這裏有舞骷髏者，笑如刑天。

一百里金粉地，他作無常傀儡戲，
我是北宋賣眼藥者，滿身眼睛過臨安，
繞而不入人血饅頭之肆。

58

9.

How sorrowful that mountains and rivers remain elegant after raising
            the price of land.
Huang Binhong and his rebels have been expelled from the country.
How sorrowful that clouds still pass through China and Jiangnan has sun
            and rain.

Survivors have no umbrellas, crossing the Su and Bai Causeways in heavy rain.
The unjust verdict from forty years ago has been completely washed away.
I take out my camera to photograph him, but only capture a blast of white

droplets. He waves his hand anxiously as a sign of rejection—
"Don't photograph me! This 2000-year-old scene is much more beautiful!"
If beauty is an accomplice, I'll simply head to Peach Blossom Island or
            Wagang Camp!


10.

It truly couldn't be more beautiful! Amazing the mountains and rivers
are not yet destroyed, but we hold luxurious grass and trees in our heart,
we swing axes at Jinming and bloodshed turns into a songbird.

Forty years ago a nameless person died in a nameless country,
something like Zhang Zhixin, Liu Hezhen or Xu Xilin,
a hundred years ago a skeleton-dancer laughed like Xing Tian.

Hundreds of miles of golden land where he stages a puppet theatre
            of impermanence,
I'm a merchant of eye-ointment in the Northern Song, covered with eyes
I go through Lin'an, I bypass but do not enter the human-blood bun market.

II.

"你們誰記得5月16日？"我在夢中怒斥，
夢中人皆歡喜，皆組織遊園會嬉戲。
一個噩夢。我也險些不能記起。

美也在修訂規矩，西湖空明，
底下有上千年的淤積：全是雲的殘骸；
而陶成章的東湖，更深百尺。

噩夢淋漓，列鬼環繞，即使遊人都爍金
也不減鬼們劍中英氣。舉國疲軟
只有他們駐足處牢如釘子，即將掀起亂世。


12.

日復一日我們看見風趟過烏雲
隨我們流亡在和平時期。鐵軌在生變、
氣流在生變、廣州深呼吸著城中村。

美也在呼聚不美：在山西仍有65人
困於煤井，他們的骨頭在黑暗中移動
發出錚錚聲響，不亞於嵇康和莊周之歌。

不美在犧牲，成爲新的美。
颱風穿過東南沿海，
嶺南的竹樹兇猛碰撞、結集。

11.

"Who remembers May 16th?" I shouted angrily in my dream,
all the others in my dream were happy and organizing games.
What a nightmare. I can barely remember.

Beauty also amends the rule: there are a thousand years of mud
beneath clear West Lake: everything becomes the remains of clouds;
the East Lake of Tao Chengzhang is one hundred meters deep.

The nightmare was vivid, ghosts surrounded me, even though visitors melted
the metal, the heroic spirits of the ghosts' swords never lowered. When the
                    entire country is exhausted and weak,
they'll stand as firm as a nail, they're ready to bring unrest.


12.

Day after day we watch the wind crossing dark clouds,
following us in exile in time of peace. Rails are shifting,
currents are shifting, Guangzhou is breathing urban villages in deeply.

Beauty collects nonbeauty: in Shanxi, 65 people are
trapped in a coal shaft, their bones move in the darkness,
clang clang, no weaker than the song of Ji Kang and Zhuang Zhou.

Nonbeauty is a sacrifice, it becomes new beauty.
A typhoon passes along the coast of Southeast China,
the bamboo trees of Lingnan clash violently then unite to become one.

# 夜中國

零星的燈火如野火
初生的或將萎的草木仍在蒙昧中起伏
總有舊雪賦予它們輪廓

我不知道這裏是河南還是湖北
只看見在路軌旁的黑暗中有一個人蹲著
他長得和我一樣，他就是我

但他的眼鏡上佈滿了劃痕
眼睛瞪得比我大，像盛滿燭光的銀碗
饑餓地在虛空中不斷掏挖

他的衣衫襤褸如這山河
在無名卷揚的烈風中哆嗦
他的手指凍成了青色，仍抓緊頑石一顆

我帶不走他，轉眼我就看不見他了
他身後是整個驟暗驟明的國度
鐵軌鋪出萬千線索，仍抓緊頑石一顆

# Night China

Scattered lights are wildfires
Newborn or withering plants rise and fall in a haze
Forever outlined in old snow

I don't know whether this is Henan or Hubei
I can only make out someone squatting in the dark next to the rail
He looks like me, he is me

His glasses are covered in scratches
His eyes stare larger than I am, like a silver bowl of candlelight
Digging hungrily in an emptiness without stopping

His clothes are as tattered as this land
He shivers in strong wind that whirls indefinably
His fingers are chilled to the bone yet stay grasped to a stone

I can't take him with me and soon I can no longer see him
Behind him the entire nation is sometimes bright sometimes dim
The rail has paved thousands of clues yet stays grasped to a stone

# 薄扶林道，尋林泉居

—— 致戴望舒

我用了一個小時在浦飛路、士美非路
尋找你的蹤跡，甚至向貓問路。
而你就一直在我身邊默默地走
彷彿在聽着雨的電台。

上坡、下坡，我只好一路向你解釋
用這苦雨斷續的頻率：
我也有寂靜的窗台和几架書
在另一個島嶼，也有一個美麗的妻子。

而現在，我們遠離了這一切和我們的時代，
打着傘，踩着遍地的影樹的影、
玉蘭樹的落英；烏云在摩星嶺上聚散，
等車的人和睡覺的貓微笑隱進了水霧里。

漫漫無盡的苦路——薄扶林，日薄
鳧歸於林，沒有此起彼落的喚友之聲，
我們又重走你走過一千遍的老路，
微雨似乎在擦亮你黯黃的煙斗。

"過了橋，"沒有橋，"走下几百的石階，"
沒有石階。但流水總是熟悉的吧！
當我抬頭看見石板上"林泉"二字，
雨突然又下得呼吸困難。

# Looking for Woodbrook Villa on Pokfulam Road

*—To Dai Wangshu*

I searched Pokfield and Pokfulam Roads for an hour,
for your footprints. I even asked a cat for directions.
You walked silently next to me along the way
like listening to a radio of rain.

All the way uphill, downhill, I'd better explain it to you
in an interrupted frequency of heavy rain:
I too have a silent windowsill and shelves of books,
I have a beautiful wife on another island.

But right now, we are far from these eras,
holding an umbrella, we step on the shadows of flamboyant trees and fallen
                    flowers of Yulan
Magnolias scattered on the ground; dark clouds gather over Mount Davis,
people wait for buses, sleeping cats smile and hide in the mist.

A bitter road with no end, Pokfulam at sunset—
wild ducks return to the woods, without the sound of calling friends,
once again walking the old paths you've crossed a thousand times,
the drizzle appears to shine your gloomy pipe.

"After you cross the bridge," there's no bridge, "go several hundred steps,"
there are no steps. But the flowing water will be familiar!
When I look up and see "Woodbrook" carved on the stone entrance,
it suddenly begins to rain so hard I can barely breathe.

密集如70年前的子彈，這廢屋也不能暫避，
山澗洶湧彷彿要給我傾出他的全部，
雨也傾出了全部的話語，
彷彿是一個和一千個幽靈在爭相傾訴。

一個工人冒着雨推門出去了，
一個女孩走進來，打開電閘，二樓就亮了一扇窗。
我站在山坡上俯瞰他們，極力看得眼睛發疼，
是酸雨滲進了我的眼膜。

但是甚麼隨着山風，揚上了合歡樹的樹梢？
是甚麼隨着驚鳥，啼鳴遠離着陸沉的小島？
園子前面的一片海，迎送過多少人的魂夢？
鬱鬱的雷聲，是盛世還是衰竭的禮炮？

"在迢遙的陽光下，也有璀璨的園林嗎？"
只是手上沒有錶，算不出暴雨的速度。
烈火打掃着天南地北的房屋，伶仃洋
另一個花園外，你探首空想着天外的主人。

我寂靜如一條被雨沖散了氣味的狗。

The rain's as intense as bullets from 70 years ago, this shack is unsuitable
                    even as temporary shelter,
the mountain stream surges like it wants to tell me everything,
the rain is spilling everything as well,
it's like one and a thousand spirits are vying to recount it all.

A worker pushes open the door and braves the rain,
a girl comes in, opens the gate; a window lights up on the second floor.
I stand on the slope and stare back at them until my eyes begin to burn,
acid rain seeping into my eyes.

But what follows the mountain breeze rises to the tips of Persian Silk trees?
What follows the frightened birds whose cries are leaving the sinking island?
How many dreams has the sea said farewell to in front of the garden?
Is the gloomy thunder a gun salute for our heyday or decline?

"Are there bright gardens beneath the distant sun?"
I don't have a watch and can't gauge the rainstorm's speed.
Raging fires sweep away houses across China. You crane your head
outside another garden at the Lingding Sea, imagine a master beyond the sky.

I'm silent as a dog whose scent has been washed away by the rain.

# 十四行

來生我願意做一個安達露西亞女子，
跳著佛拉明高撕碎、拋散自己的一片海。

或者庫爾德高地上的一株櫻桃樹，
看著黑馬來去、花瓣落向老詩人的窗戶。

要么乾脆是塔爾寺上空的一朵雲，
清淨空中的微雷、旋生旋滅的咒語。

現在我是空餘鐵甲的騎兵，在中國東北
枕戈待旦，聽聞怒雪落滿了黃河以南。

就像上個世紀一個叛變的白俄，流放營中
聽那年輕的西亞人回憶他的妻子和烏德琴。

八千人在積雪上灑著工業鹽，八個電工
在冰封的電塔上過冬，再也不下來這莽莽人間。

我空餘鐵甲、孤獨魚的鱗片——
一片作爲燒水的烙鐵，另一片徹夜敲響。

# Sonnet

In the next life I want to be an Andalusian woman,
dancing a flamenco that tears and scatters into her own sea.

Or a cherry tree in Kurdish highlands,
Watching black horses come and go, petals falling onto
                    an old poet's window.

Or simply a cloud over Kumbum Monastery,
bursts of thunder in a clear sky and curses passing in an instant.

Now I'm a cavalry soldier with nothing but my armor in Northeast China
ready for battle and waiting for dawn, hearing heavy snow has covered
                    the Yellow River's southern stretch.

Like a White Russian guerilla from the last century, in a labor camp,
listening to a young man from Western Asia remembering his wife and oud.

Eight thousand people sprinkle industrial salt on snow, eight electricians
spend the winter in a frozen electrical tower, never to return to this
                    white endless world.

I have nothing but my armor, the scales of a lonely fish—
One section used as an iron for boiling water, another as an alarm
                    sounding through the night.

# 重訪杜甫草堂

舊時蘊慰能傷心，
假風物亦能傷心。
杜甫不再等於本地，
只吹噓一地竹殼。

然而春風也怒號，
狼藉人裝上了刺刀。
我拖這空箱搬運咄咄，
黑石唯認得唐音。

惡睡者做了個錯夢，
夢得她照鏡，爲做夢人驚。
滿城颯颯，黃四娘如雲。

唯其銅像已鏽，丹妝
不再含西嶺、也不飛鴻。
故紙拒簽了故國。

# Revisiting Du Fu's Thatched Cottage

Ancient consolation can be heartbreaking,
artificial scenery also can be heartbreaking.
Du Fu no longer epitomizes this place,
bragging over bamboo husks on the ground.

Yet a spring breeze roars furiously,
people in disarray fitting their bayonets.
I drag an empty suitcase over cobble
black stones that only know Tang sounds.

The insomniac had the wrong dream,
in which she looks into a mirror, terrified
              by the dreamer's own face.
The entire city is bustling, full of Auntie Huangs.

His bronze statue has rusted, the red makeup
no longer contains the western hills, or a flying swan.
Ancient letters refuse entry to the ancient land.

# 拉薩來信

你路過了長江，浪花
仍然在漩渦中游泳；
你的火車已經到達江西，
陽光和桃樹仍然種遍了山野。

但這裏，拉薩早已合上了她的夜幕
在沸騰的海幡裏，在煙火熏黑
的鳥巢裏，在孩子籠入袖中的
金色小髒手裏。拉薩的鳥以甚麼爲食？

2.

小卓瑪的窗子關不上
在風中不停地唱：一條路
穿過沖賽康，沒有盡頭，四通八達
奔跑的青年將在這裏流盡了汗。

拉薩早已合上了她的夜幕。
火星跳起來，在每個人額上烙印；
你路過了拉薩，路過沖賽康，
你吃的青稞面是苦的，你手中也有火星一枚。

# A Letter from Lhasa

1.

You've crossed over the Yangtze; spindrifts
still swirl in a pool;
your train's arrived in Jiangxi,
sunshine and peach trees spread over mountains and plains.

But here in Lhasa the curtain of night's already fallen
in a boiling sea of flags, in a smoky black bird's
nest, in a child's small hands, golden,
filthy and shrouded in sleeves. What do birds eat in Lhasa?

2.

Little Dolma's window won't shut, it's
singing relentlessly in the wind: An endless road
passing through Tromsikhang heads in all directions;
dashing youths sweat profusely.

In Lhasa the curtain of night's already fallen.
Sparks flare up and leave a mark on each forehead;
you passed through Lhasa, through Tromsikhang,
the barley noodles you ate were bitter, a spark in your hand.

# 宇宙大苦行詩

—1月16日，香港反高鐵人民在立法會即將通過高鐵撥
款表決之時，發起萬人宇宙大苦行、包圍立法會，
悲且壯，詩以記之。

I.

熔岩漸漸流緩、變黑，
我們拖著熔岩走路。
宇宙在苦行
一萬人在轉，因為腳下星也轉
不因愚政而停止。

金剛攀上了立法會
不作獅吼，只結一個寂靜手印。
正義女神依然蒙眼
他們相愛進入高空凜冽
高空還有銀河如幡。

我們匍匐在冰冷瀝青上
雙膝護住地底一團火。
青色火，燒成一條悲傷的蛇
警卒們的離魂如尺蠖
去追，總追不著。

戰城南、死城北，精衛
不再填海，裸身走在立法會
肥議員們染了一身幽寒。
宇宙在苦行
席捲了世間狼藉酒杯。

76

# Poem for the Universe's Prostrating-Walk

—On 16 January 2010, as the Legislative Council was preparing to approve the funding application for the Guangzhou-Shenzhen-Hong Kong Express Rail Link, a group of Hong Kong citizens opposed to the measure surrounded the Legislative Council building in a ten-thousand-person Prostrating-Walk.

I.

Lava flows gradually slow and turn black,
we walk dragging along the lava.
The universe's prostrating-walk,
ten thousand people turn as the planet turns beneath
not to be halted by inane policies.

King Kong climbs the Legislative Council
without a roar. He makes a mudra in silence.
Lady Justice is still wearing her blindfold.
They fall in love and enter a frozen sky,
the Milky Way flaps in the sky.

We crawl on cold bitumen,
our knees protecting an underground fire.
Green fire burns into a sad snake,
ghost soldiers soul's are like looping inchworms
that chase after but never catch them.

Battling in the south of the city, dying in the north, Jingwei
no longer fills the sea, she walks nude into the Legislative Council.
The fat councilors have caught a chill.
The universe's prostrating-walk,
scattered wine cups around the world.

## 2.

它如一株巨樹，
高舉全身花瓣，在黑暗中攀緣
吞沒奮戰於子夜的人和獸，
湧上上亞厘畢道、翻下戾臣道。
這夜，我擁護地心說。

是宇宙在敲鼓、在胡旋、
在二十六步一跪拜、攢緊手中穀，
是它突然奮起如日冕、
兀而俯身如星雲，
全身的枝葉垂下、包裹一個小村。

再無所謂高官與碩鼠的齗齗，
光流布了路砂的細隙
它要回它施予的一切
準備一場豐收宴。
我們如勞農作歌，高空還有銀河。

宇宙在苦行
爲了一個老婦人的念叨，
她和它相依爲命已經八十年
仍將延續數億光年。
爲她暫寐，我撚熄這顆小星。

2.

It's like a huge tree,
upholds all the petals, climbs in darkness,
swallows humans and beasts battling at midnight,
rising to Albert Road, rolling down to Jackson.
Tonight I support a geocentric theory.

It's the universe which hits the drum, dances,
prostrates itself every twenty-six steps, holds grains tightly in its hands,
quickly rising like a solar corona,
then bending down like a nebula,
all the branches and leaves hang down, wrap up a small village.

No more teeth and gums of so-called high officials and giant rats,
light spreads through every tiny crack in the road,
claiming all it gives
in preparation for a celebration of a good harvest.
We sing like farmers, the Milky Way is in the sky.

The universe's prostrating-walk
for an old woman's repeated words
have depended on each other's survival for eighty years
and will go on for several billion light years.
For the sake of her brief sleep, I stub out this little star.

# 耶穌在廟街（阿云的聖誕歌）

耶穌在廟街，阿云在耶路撒冷。
在耶路撒冷做甚麼？一坐下就哭。

哭甚麼？今天被警察幹，
幹了我還要遞押我出境。

哭甚麼？今天被"大佬"幹，
幹了我還搶去我一千塊錢。

今天那可以做我爺爺的老頭他壓在我身上，
今天那記者、法官、署長他們壓在我身上。

阿云你撒謊，你不在耶路撒冷，
你分明在香港。

耶穌也不在廟街，
他在九龍灣，做些地盤的黑工。

偶爾抬頭，想起了伯利恆。
想起伯利恆做甚麼？等待一顆星。

阿云在廟街，從左走到右，從右走到左。
地球在她腳下轉着，摩擦着她：

從里到外，從身到心。它粗礪得可怕
一如兩千零六年前那個聖誕夜，

# Jesus Is on Temple Street (A-yun's Christmas Song)

Jesus is on Temple Street, A-yun is in Jerusalem.
What are you doing in Jerusalem? She cries as she sits down.

What are you crying for? I was fucked over by a cop today,
he fucked me and deported me.

What are you crying for? I was fucked by my boss today.
He fucked me and then stole a thousand dollars from me.

Today that old man who could be my grandfather screwed me.
Today that reporter, judge and government officer screwed me.

A-yun you're lying. You're not in Jerusalem.
You're definitely in Hong Kong.

Jesus is not on Temple Street either.
He's in Kowloon Bay, working illegally on construction sites.

Sometimes he looks up and thinks of Bethlehem.
Why are you thinking of Bethlehem? Waiting for a star.

A-yun is on Temple Street, walking from left to right, from right to left.
The earth is turning under her feet, rubbing against her:

From inside out, body to mind. It's so rough it's scary,
like Christmas Eve 2006 years ago.

一顆星在兩千光年外爆炸、毀滅，
彼時，耶穌在廟街，阿云又名抹大拉。

抹大拉又名瑪利亞。瑪利亞的兒子在伯利恆，
阿云的兒子在四川鄉下。

A star exploded and was destroyed 2000 light years away.
Back then, Jesus was on Temple Street, A-yun was known as Magdalene.

Magdalene is also known as Mary. Mary's son is in Bethlehem.
A-yun's son is in rural Sichuan.

## 鹿鳴街·獻給胡婆婆

這里只是馬頭角道無數伸向東面
的小巷中的一條，擠滿了密匝匝的唐樓，
沒有電梯，樓梯也布滿積水，
因為它的窗戶沒有玻璃，引入橫街上潑來的全部風雨。

但這沒關係，樓下排列成行的汽車維修店沒關係，
對面的牛棚藝術村沒關係，北面的山南面的海
都沒關係，即使香港不是香港
而只是無數荒涼唐樓中一座，都和你沒關係。

八月雨暫時停止，陽光剎那猛烈，
你拉上拼湊的布簾子，下午的酷熱仍然鑽進來。
七樓上你又租到一個簡陋的房間暫居，
因為你居港不夠七年，他們把你從公屋趕出來。

這沒關係，你的世界，從1952年的冬至夜開始
已經自己攜帶，廣州到武漢，武漢到廣州；
他的世界也自己攜帶着，大街到監獄，監獄到大街，
1952年的冬至夜，他的詩也一直攜帶着那一夜。

1996年，他終於不勝重負。從此兩個世界都壓向
你消瘦的兩肩，像魔力伸進了你的兩手，
你停不下來寫寫寫，從廣州到香港，從黃大仙公屋

# Luk Ming Street: To Madame Wu

This is one of the many lanes along Ma Tau Kok Road
that stretches to the east, densely placed tenements
with no lifts and flooded stairs
because the windows have no glass, so the rain pours in from the alley.

But it doesn't really matter; the strip of downstairs garages doesn't matter,
the Cattle Depot Artist Village across the street doesn't matter,
the mountains in the north or sea in the south
doesn't matter either. Even Hong Kong is not Hong Kong
and only one of these desolate tenements doesn't matter to you.

In August the rains stop for a while, the sun suddenly shines.
You close the pieced together curtains but the afternoon heat seeps through.
You've rented a spare room on the 7th floor.
They drove you out of public housing because you'd been in Hong Kong
                less than seven years.

But it doesn't matter. Your world, which began the evening of the 1952 winter
solstice, has carried you from Guangzhou to Wuhan, Wuhan to Guangzhou;
his world has carried him too, from street to prison, from prison to street.
Since that winter solstice in 1952, his poems have carried that night.

He finally succumbed to the burden in 1996. From that time on the two
                worlds have pressed
down on your thin shoulders, your hands empowered by magic.
You write, write, write endlessly, from Guangzhou to Hong Kong, from
                public housing in Wong Tai Sin

到鹿鳴街閣樓，熄燈后，兩個世界同時顯靈。

兩個世界終於疊合成一個，你忍耐了几十年，
這個戰鬥着的世界凌越了窗外狹窄的鹿鳴街
和更狹窄的香港。每一個字都戰鬥着，
夜夜招來風雨、鬼魅，時而耳語，時而厲喊。

鹿鳴街的街坊，誰也看不見你帶着這麼巨大的一個戰場
每天清晨靜靜步下一百多級樓梯，
去九龍城碼頭晨運、到街市買菜、來往死生之間
鹿鳴街樓梯口一堵鐵門，死生唯一一道簡單的縫隙。

如果你願意，你就是鹿鳴街的毛特·崗，英姿颯爽。
但不是，你更願意在此崢嶸世界呦呦鹿鳴、食野之萍，
這也是他的夢想、我的夢想。為此我們躍過
葉芝的湖澤，回到魯迅的荒郊、長夜春時、煉獄。

用墨凍如鐵的毛筆，用南囚的鉛筆，用你今天
陌生摸索的電腦輸入法，你們都固執地寫及
東方既白。雖然鹿鳴街窗戶對面仍是窗戶，

to the mezzanine level at Luk Ming Street; after switching off the light
        the two worlds appear together.

The two worlds finally become one. You've endured it all for decades.
This battling world has gone past the narrow stretch of Luk Ming Street
        beyond the window
and the even narrower Hong Kong. Each word is a struggle;
every night brings wind and rain, ghosts and goblins, sometimes a whisper,
        sometimes a shout.

Nobody on Luk Ming Street can see the immense battlefield you carry
each morning quietly walking down one hundred stairs to exercise
at Kowloon City Pier, to the market for groceries, traveling the staircase between
life and death through the iron gate at Luk Ming Street, a simple slot between
        life and death.

If you're willing, you could become the Maud Gonne of Luk Ming  Street,
        bold and brave.
But no, you'd rather be a deer in this memorable world, so you can bleat
        loudly and eat in the wild.
This is his dream, as well as mine, for which we've leapt across
Yeat's lake, and returned to Lu Xun's barren countryside, a long spring night
        of purgatory.

With brushes as cold as iron, imprisoned pencils, with the unfamiliar Chinese
input methods for today's computers, both of you stubbornly write until
the sun rises in the east. Although the windows of Luk Ming street peer out
        on other windows,

香港的樓阻擋着樓，中國的日出只照耀浦東的少數⋯⋯

但1952年，冬至夜，你們唱起了違禁的《國際歌》，
一直違禁，一直沉吟至今。鹿鳴街，月明星稀，
鹿游蕩於天台樓燠熱未退的鐵皮屋頂上、魚骨天線間，
低頭嗅你慣於孤獨的青青衣衿。

buildings in Hong Kong obstruct other buildings, the sunrise in China only
                    shines on a few in Pudong . . .

Yet on that winter solstice eve in 1952, you sang the banned Internationale.
You've hummed it from the moment it was banned. At Luk Ming Street,
                    the moon is bright and stars are few;
deer wander between the hot iron rooftops and fishbone antennas,
lower their heads to sniff your lonely green clothes.

# 中環天星碼頭歌謠

"黑夜里的謊言他們白天說，他們早上說
中午說在大氣電波里說在金色帷幕背后咬耳朵說
他們說他們說。潔白的骨骼他們黑夜里拆，
他們黃昏拆他們早上拆他們侮辱着晨光拆他們
在黑犬的保護下拆在海風的沉默下拆他們拆他們拆。"

我是49歲的碼頭我在嚴寒中搖着頭，
我搖着頭摸着肋間的傷口看着政府里的孫子們擦着手，
我搖着頭一任尖叫的海鷗點數我的骨頭，
我端出了一盆血給這些孫子洗手，洗他們烏黑的手，
我敲打着大鐘的最后一個齒輪唱着49年前的歌謠：

"呵雨水淌過我的前額我看見對岸的火車站多麼遙遠
多麼遙遠，它終將消失不見終化成維港上空一縷煙；
呵雨水淌過我的胸膛我的心臟，我看見維港越來越瘦
越來越瘦，它終將消失不見終變成售價十元的一張明信片，
這香港終將消失不見終變成一個無限期還款的樓盤。"

"雨水呵我的妹妹我的證人，現在請輕柔地拭去
我身上的瓦礫它們硌得我生痛，請輕柔地拭去這49年
我身上的腳印、戀人們的身影、那些呢喃的夢話和鐘聲……
請輕柔地安慰這些為我哭泣的年輕人，讓他們帶走我的每一塊鐵
為了日后的鬥爭。"

# Ballad of the Central Star Ferry Pier

"During the day they tell the night's lies, they tell them at morning
at noon in atmospheric waves behind gold curtains they whisper into ears
they tell and they tell. White skeletons demolished at night,
demolished at dusk demolished at dawn they humiliate the dawn
and demolish, protected by black dogs they demolish in the silence of the
sea breeze they demolish, demolish."

I'm a 49-year-old pier shaking my head in the cold,
shaking my head I touch the wound between my ribs, I watch the government
                       bastards rub their hands,
shaking my head as the screaming gulls count my bones
taking out a bucket of blood so these bastards can wash their hands, wash
                       their black hands,
I strike the last gear of the clock and sing a ballad from 49 years ago:

"Ah the rain drips on my forehead, I can see the train station across
the harbour far far away far far away; it will finally disappear it will vanish
into the smoke into the sky over Victoria Harbour. Ah the rain drips on my
chest on my heart I watch Victoria Harbour grow thinner and thinner,
thinner and thinner. It all will finally disappear to become a postcard sold
for ten dollars. This Hong Kong will disappear and become real property
with an unspecified mortgage."

"The rain, ah my darling, my witness, please gently wipe away the debris
on me is pressing down so painfully; please wipe away the 49 years
of footprints, lovers' silhouettes, all those murmured delusions and bells . . .
please comfort these young people crying for me. Let them take
all my iron for their future struggles."

# 野蠻夜歌

火車越挨近北方的青你越遠
這是突瓦這是烏蘭巴托

我越是狂奔大路越是不見
這是風飄著刀這是雪灑下的劍

馬群亂，馬背上是悲傷的大軍
醉蹄下踐踏著我銀的嗓音

突瓦的啞巴，也比夜鶯婉轉
烏蘭巴托的夜，卻那么靜那么靜

我穿越中國又一夜又一個時代漠漠
就像千年前失敗的完顏

整個中國都熄滅了烤焦了
只有隧道裏有光，也被我一口口吃掉

蒙古利亞兀自跳著野蠻的舞
野蠻但是腰間的酒瓶叮噹響

我將於明晨來到你草原的邊緣
那裏雙聲渾濁那裏長調截斷

那裏是北京那個破城啊
可汗悲傷的大軍、瘋狂的大軍曾經佔領。

# A Barbarous Night Song

The nearer my train gets to the northern green the farther away you are
This is Tuva this is Ulan Bator

The wilder I run the harder it is to see the road
This is a sabre in the wind this is a sword in the snow

Horses run wild with a sorrowful army on their backs
Drunken hooves are trampling my silver voice

Mutes in Tuva sweeter than nightingales
Nights in Ulan Bator ever so quiet

I pass through China, another night another era, vast and lonely
Like the Khan of the Jurchens conquered a thousand years ago

The whole of China is burned and scorched
There's only light in the tunnel, which is eaten by me

Mongolia keeps dancing its barbarous steps
Barbarous but with jingling wine flasks tied to waists

By tomorrow morning I'll be on the edge of your steppes
Where the sounds of the Hoomii muddy, where long song music is cut off

That's Beijing, the broken city
Once occupied by the great Khan's sorrowful unbridled army.

## 巴黎暴動歌謠

現在數一、二、三，
讓我們把巴黎掀翻重來，
爲地下鐵、地下人和地下鬼排演喜劇。
就從索邦開始，掀去牆上的選舉招貼
找出彈痕和血迹；掀翻萬聖殿
從門票裏解放狄德羅；拆下蓬比杜的彩色管子
分發到每雙憤怒的手上，讓暴力更美，
讓我們敲打彼此的腦袋激發月光曲。
歌唱塞納河上空的鴿子飛來飛去無法著地，
它們的沉默也足以致死。

讓我們把巴黎打到1968年之前去，
此後的巴黎不是巴黎；
讓我們把巴黎公社的斷牆
從拉雪茲公墓拉回巴士底，拆成磚石
重砌街壘。你的弟弟妹妹們
已經在遊行的佇列裏
他們將把奧塞美術館的僞中國畫撕成粉碎。
釋放郊區的阿拉伯人、阿拉伯數字；
考核遊客和移民們的想象力，
讓他們的美元、歐元和人民幣見鬼去。
歌唱塞納河上空的鴿子飛來飛去無法著地，
它們的沉默也足以致死。

我們撕碎巴黎的雨，代之以雪塊，
讓巴黎的雲穿上流浪漢的褲子；
奧蒂昂廣場上的大學生也應該有蘭波的蝨子，

# Ballad of the Paris Uprising

Let us count one, two, three,
overturn Paris and start again,
rehearse a subway comedy, underground people, underground ghosts.
Let us start with the Sorbonne, tear the election posters from the walls
search for bullet scars and bloodstains. Overturn the Panthéon,
free Diderot's image on tickets. Tear down the Pompidou's colorful pipes
distribute them to each angry hand, let violence become more beautiful;
let us smash each other's heads to rouse the *Moonlight Sonata*.
Chanting pigeons fly back and forth over the Seine, unable to land;
their silence is enough to kill.

Let us attack Paris, return to the pre-1968 era,
Paris after then is not Paris.
Let us pull down the Commune's broken walls,
from Père Lachaise Cemetery to the Bastille, break into bricks and stone,
rebuild the barricades. Your younger brothers and sisters
are already on the march.
They will shred the fake Chinese paintings in Musée d'Orsay.
Release the Arabs and Arabic numerals in the suburbs;
test the imagination of tourists and migrants,
to hell with their Dollars, Euros and Yuan.
Chanting pigeons fly back and forth over the Seine, unable to land;
their silence is enough to kill.

We shred the rain in Paris, replace it with blocks of snow,
let the clouds in Paris don a vagrant's pants;
university students at the Place d'Odéon should have Rimbaud's lice,

把蒙馬特還給辛勤的妓女，
讓她們沖國際藝術家婊子們吐口水，
把街頭還給戈達爾，把詩歌還給政治。
星月在轉，這裏也不過是小小寰宇，
歡迎搶掠，我兜裏有的是鮑狄埃的詩句。
歌唱塞納河上空的鴿子飛來飛去無法著地，
它們的沉默也足以致死。

return Montmartre to the hardworking hookers,
let them spit at the international artist bitches,
return the streets to Godard, return poetry to politics.
Stars and moon rise and set, this is just a tiny earth;
looting is welcome, I have Pottier's poems in my pocket.
Chanting pigeons fly back and forth over the Seine, unable to land;
their silence is enough to kill.

# 灰心謠

他一寸寸埋葬自己，
至今已三十三年;
但是海風仍然快樂地繞著他打轉。

認識三年的樓下保安員，
今夜相當詫異:
他又變回一個長著鯰魚頭的單身漢。

他耳機裡痙攣的"電台司令"
十年沒聽，今夜又痛擊他
像一粒酒精。

久未謀面的老友，昨晚大笑
因為他還為了格瓦拉之死未獲道歉
而拒絕美國簽證。

"一切就像十年前，但你更左了！"
不，他的右在吃著他的左，
他的左又吃著他的右。

還有那些曾一起在雪地裡走失的人，
被紛飛雪球打得暈頭轉向，
以後再也見不到的人。

他們在蒙昧中虛構著這一個他，
他們用大麻葉蘸著虛空，
草草的回憶起他。

# Ballad of Disheartenment

For thirty-three years
he's buried himself inch by inch,
yet the sea breeze still wraps happily around him.

The security guard he's known for three years
is startled by him tonight:
he's newly single and grown a catfish head.

Radiohead's spastic in his ear,
idling for ten years, it hits him as hard tonight
as grain alcohol.

An old friend no one's seen for years howls the whole night,
still refusing to apply for a U.S. visa
because they never apologized for the death of Che Guevara.

"Everything's like it was ten years ago, except you're more of a leftist!"
No, his right is eating his left
while his left eats his right.

There were people who wandered into a snow-filled landscape
and were hit with snowballs, confused and disoriented,
after which they were never seen again.

In their ignorance, they fictionalized "him."
They dipped hemp leaves into nihilism,
remembering him with a nonchalance.

在海風中撿回他的鼻子，
在電波中撈出他的耳朵，
在月光中描繪出他的眼睛……

然而他曾經用這些東西一起說：
我愛。他曾經把地球點燃，
看它燒成一個薔薇花蕾。

就讓打鐘的打鐘，看雲的看雲，
他一寸寸埋葬自己，
至今已三十三年。

From the sea breeze his nose was collected,
from electric waves his ears were dredged,
from the moonlight his eyes were drawn . . .

Yet he once used all of these together to say:
I love. He once lit up the earth
and watched it burn into a rose bud.

Let those who are tolling toll, let those who are seeing clouds see,
for thirty-three years
he's buried himself inch by inch.

## 錄鬼簿・海子
### （詩人，死於1989年3月26日）

我死於死亡之前，洪水
提前分開了我，列車
只經過我的血跡，只帶走
我的饑餓，推向燦爛的湖面。

如今我就是大湖上栽種幻像的那人，
我就是把鐵軌一一引入水面的野花中
的那人。我滿目都是生命
像把臉埋入野花中的山羊。

洪水從山海關流漫到龍家營，
那是子夜一點。哦，黑夜
請原諒我的詩一點也不晦澀，
請原諒這身衣服，比黎明更藍。

如今我聽見七十天後的槍聲只是寂靜，
我看見二十年後的塗鴉只是潔淨。
那些攜帶我的死亡到處行走的人
他們是一隊蜻蜓。

那路上的青草盡枯！紅鏽
混入了泥土！我手捧一堆漢字：
一堆"生存"的同義詞，
在黎明的微寒中燒掉了紙做的衣服。

# Register of Ghosts: Haizi
(Died March 26, 1989)

I died before death, the flood
separated me early, the train
only passed over my bloodstains, only took
my starvation, pushed towards a glorious lake.

Today I am that person planting fantasies on the lake,
I am drawing the rails one by one into the wild flowers on the lake,
that person. Life is all around me
like a mountain goat with its face buried in wildflowers.

The water slowly floods from Shanhaiguan to Longjiaying,
just after midnight. Oh, black night
forgive my song's lack of subtlety,
forgive the clothes on this body, bluer even than dawn.

Today I only hear silence after seventy days of shooting,
I only see purity after twenty years of graffiti.
Those who carry my death wherever they go
are dragonflies.

The green grass on the road is dry to the tip! Red rust
blends into the soil! A pile of characters in both hands:
a pile of synonyms for "survival,"
in the gentle cold of dawn I burned paper clothing.

洪水從苜蓿地流漫到汐止門，
那是凌晨三點。哦，黑夜
請原諒我的詩一點也不悲傷，
請原諒這身衣服，比黎明更貴重。

The water floods from Muxudi to Xizhimen,
three in the morning. Oh, black night
forgive the lack of grief in my song,
forgive the clothes on this body, more valuable even than dawn.

# 錄鬼簿・駱一禾

（詩人，1989年5月13日因參與絕食在廣場暈倒，昏迷18天，5月31日於天壇醫院去世，可能是「六四」運動的第一個死者）


熱風剎那抱緊我的頭顱，親愛的
我仍記得，這腥甜屬於海，
不屬於廣場上金色塵土。然後
我便在二十年黑河中擺渡亡靈。

十八天昏睡中升起我的渴，親愛的
我仍記得，熱風穿上了你的連衣裙，
裏面是裸體燙滾。然後船舷下
酒醉的泳者，為我卯緊了星星的柳釘。

是我從他胃裏撿起那兩個橘子，
從他的動脈裏撈起一株向日葵。
是我向廣場投下日晷般長影，
為你們、還有他們，最後一次校準時間。

請叫喚我的名字：卡戎。黑夜裏
是誰血流披面？我情願這染紅的
是我的白衫——請原諒這一身衣服
比原諒更輕，比死更晶瑩。

親愛的，我愛上了這最後的鐘聲，
它在每一個死者的血管裏繼續轟鳴。
今夜是詩歌最後一次獲得光榮！
而我們將第二次穿過同一個深淵。

# Register of Ghosts: Luo Yihe

*(A poet who joined the hunger strike on Tiananmen Square and collapsed on May 13, 1989. He fell into a coma before dying in the hospital on May 31, 1989. Luo was possibly the first victim of the June Fourth incident. )*

A hot wind engulfed my head, my dear,
I still remember the bloody smell of the sea,
not from gold dust on the square. For the past
twenty years I've been helping dead souls cross the Heihe.

An eighteen-day waking sleep increased my thirst, my dear,
I still remember how the hot wind dressed you,
your nude body boiling inside. Then beneath the gunnel
a drunken swimmer tightly screwed in fasteners for me.

It was me who picked two tangerines from his stomach,
who dredged a sunflower from his artery.
It was me who cast a long shadow in the square like a sundial,
for you, and for them, to adjust the time of day one last time.

Please call my name: Charon. Whose face is
bleeding in the dark of night? I wished the red
was on my white shirt—please forgive these clothes—
lighter than forgiveness, more translucent than death.

My dear, I was in love with the final tolling bell,
it kept thundering in the blood vessels of the departed.
Tonight poetry attains its ultimate glory!
And we will pass through the same abyss a second time.

隨後是磬擊四記。軋軋的鐵履不是一次筆誤！
不是和我無關！魚們眼窩裏的青銅
不再夢見地安門。請叫喚我的名字——
我不是你的愛人，我是水中折斷的旗桿。

What followed were the sounds of stone chimes.
The squeaking iron shoes were not just a slip of the pen!
They were not irrelevant to me! Bronze in the fish eyes
no longer dreamt of Di'anmen. Please, call my name—
I am not your lover, I am a broken flagstaff in the water.

# 錄鬼簿・你
（給所有死於1989年6月4日的無名者）


我靜懸在安哥拉山脈上空
不再能承擔你這第二人稱的重量：

我飛過鍍銀的大湖，眾雲在垂釣，
繼而流變，證明這是地球：一顆星。

你死於其上，死得其所。那一天
沒有風，沒有雲，細微的一聲雷也被你帶去。

你仍能記住這星球上溝壑縱橫，
如枯筆墨，舔之舌頭有血。

於是你的死不是某個人的死，
你倒下激起的塵埃將使空氣中飽含了雨的分子。

一箭一箭，我是波音777中一朵枯萎
的薔薇，期待你把我射下來。

光芒乍現，我是躬耕它的犁。
空弦在夜機腹中響起。亂雲不肯和諧。

# Register of Ghosts: You
(To all the nameless who died in the June Fourth incident)


I'm suspended over an Angolan mountain range
unable to withstand the weight of you, the second person pronoun:

I'm flying over an enormous silver-plated lake, clouds are fishing,
then transform, proving it's a sphere: a star.

You died upon it, a good place to die. No wind
or clouds that day; faint thunder taken along with you.

You recalled crisscrossing ravines across the stars,
like a withered writing brush, licked by a blood-stained tongue.

So, your death is not just anyone's,
your collapse invokes the dust, saturating the air with rain molecules.

Arrow for arrow, I'm a withered rose in a Boeing 777,
waiting for you to shoot me down.

Brilliant rays suddenly appear, I'm working the plough.
Open strings are played across the belly of an evening flight.
The disordered clouds refuse all harmony.

# 一九六七，五四遺事

如果猛火還有餘燼
餘燼將散聚一幅枯山水
許是雪景，那人落落穿行去
不辨清白，不辨川壑

窄長中國，無橋無塔
也無旗幟垂落
包裹被熱風破開的振臂
飛廉戰鬥著窮奇

有人吃德賽，有人吃主義
你吃臭豆腐玉米麵糊糊
紅樓虛構了赤都
你不虛構廢姓外骨

仍有遊行佇列，你仍第一次
碰觸那溫濕的戰馬的臉
那分明是尼采的血
你們認作飼馬草上的露

如果死者還在
你們將用隱語交易一回：
這妙皺的奇嶺你袖去
這凍凝的小河我帶走。

# 1967, May Fourth Memorabilia

If embers remained after a raging fire
they would scatter and gather, forming into an arid landscape
Perhaps a snowscape, a man walked through snow
unable to distinguish transparency or whiteness, rivers or valleys

China was long and narrow, with no bridge or pagoda,
no flag hung down
Wrapping the upstretched arms opened by a hot wind
Fei Lian battled Qiong Qi

Someone ate democracy and science, someone ate an -ism
you ate stinky tofu with mashed corn
The red chamber fabricated a red Yan'an
you did not fabricate Haisei Gaikotsu

There was a parade, you touched
the warhorse's wet face the first time
That is clearly Nietzsche's blood
which you all regard as dew on fodder

If the dead were still here
you would use sign language for deals:
You tuck the chapped mountain ridge inside your sleeve
I take away the tiny frozen river.

# 海濱墓園（三首）

──為蕭紅、戴望舒、張愛玲的淺水灣而作

## 曾經的墓前：蕭紅

麗都酒店門前北行一百七十步
轉身向南，我短暫的安息處
夜仍繼續著夜，太陽也繼續每日
從涵蘊著死之繁種的海上升出
鳥翅初舉，輕理毛羽
而我已不說話。

暴風是否也繼續著暴風？
已經不再把我打擾
孩子們坐在深深的骨灰之上
聽老師講過去的事情
我銜一枚松子
饒有興味看這一切。

沒有風，烈日翻煎著海灘上
彼此陌生的情人們
我也終於看見情人盡荒涼
灰髮自輕揚
海深處萬物競生
麗都酒店反覆成為新的工場。

工場內建築工人午休
致電與他天水圍的妻兒們
今天是怎樣的午餐

# A Seaside Graveyard: Three Poems

*The Repulse Bay of Xiao Hong, Dai Wangshu and Eileen Chang*

## In Front of a Grave: Xiao Hong

From the Cosmopolitan Hotel I take 170 steps north
then turn south; night in my temporary resting place
is still night, the sun still rises everyday
from the sea which contains a million kinds of death,
birds begin to raise their wings, preening feathers
Yet I'm no longer talking.

Is the storm still raging?
It can't disturb me anymore
The children sit on deeply buried bone ash
listening to the teacher talking about the past
as I hold a pine nut in my mouth
watching it all with amusement.

There's no wind, the burning sun scorches
lovers who don't know each other on the beach
and I finally see the lovers who use up bleakness
with drifting grey hair
deep in the sea all things compete for survival,
the Cosmopolitan Hotel is always under construction.

A construction worker at noon break
calls his wife and children in Tin Shui Wai
to talk about today's lunch

樹影兒是否遮過了曬衣的窗欄
我在細沙上寫下又抹去這閒話
天邊外，野鴿飛不到呼蘭。

那裏有我純白的塑像
如用黑瓶子裏半滿的骨灰堆成
細沙流過鐵路橋和教堂
堅硬不同這裏，暮色封鎖的海和天
黎明時留連的人影已經不見——
這裏有一束紅山茶。


## 傾城之戀的舞台：張愛玲

野火花為嚴冬而燒
春天擁擠的儘是亡靈
她偷了明月的殘光下山去後
淺水灣酒店死了多少男女
他們在遺忘的錦灰堆中交媾
臉上滿是皎如珠玉的微笑。

這些瓦礫似的婚姻是昂貴的
無論是今天，還是戰時
她抱緊的一瓶牛乳也是昂貴的
刺激了多少臨終之眼
在臨時醫院，當她凌晨驚醒
才發覺抱緊的是無用的助產鉗。

像淺水灣酒店的波斯掛毯
風兒鑽過它被流彈擊穿的孔眼
青黃的山麓緩緩地暗了下來
不是因為風吹著樹

Does the tree's shadow cover the window frames of drying clothes
I write gossip in the sand and erase it again
on the horizon, wild pigeons are unable to fly to Hulan.

There is a pure white statue of me
like a pile of bone ash filling up half the black bottle,
fine sand drifting through the railway bridge and chapel
A different type of hardness is no longer the same here, where sea
                     and sky are sealed off by twilight
people wandering at dawn have left—
here is a bunch of red camellia.

### A Stage for *Love in a Fallen City*: Eileen Chang

Sparks of wildfire burn in a harsh winter,
the spirit of the deceased crowds into spring
after she steals the remaining moonlight and comes down
countless men and women die in the Repulse Bay Hotel
They copulate in forgotten piles of brocade dust,
their faces full of smiles, bright pearls and jades.

These rubbish marriages were expensive,
whether today or at wartime
the bottle of milk she held tight was also expensive,
irritating the eyes of so many dying people
in a temporary hospital, waking with a start in the wee hours
she found herself grasping a midwife's useless forceps.

Wind blew through the stray bullet holes
like a Persian tapestry in the Repulse Bay Hotel,
yellow green trees in the mountain grew dark,

也不是雲影飄移著無數
而是她突然看不清楚這小路。

二十二歲，香港淪陷，她已老
拿起筆就已經老成了
輾轉洛杉磯汽車旅館間的老婦
空幻中捉虱的孤獨
其實等同於野火花下互相驅蚊一夢
又是多少都市傾覆換得。

如今這樹重又喚成影樹
繼續為無情的過客而扶疏
只有她的鬼魂不再回來這裏
藉口是這裏有過最圓滿的結局
那堵極高極高的牆深夜裏還能看見
風沒有因為月光變成蟠龍。


**蕭紅墓畔的守夜：戴望舒**

走六小時寂寞的長途
這裏適合做你的墓地
你是羞澀的逝者
戰爭沒有了，怨恨沒有了
連寫一首四行詩的字詞都沒有了
你來到這裏坐下，像一把煙斗。

夜氣混凝，全世界都來到這裏
成為黑夜的一部分
你坐在其中，因為一束紅山茶

not from wind blowing through the trees
or countless floating clouds
but because she suddenly couldn't see the road clearly.

At twenty-two, occupied Hong Kong, she was already old,
picking up a pen she was already too mature,
an old lady of Los Angeles wandering between motels;
the loneliness of catching lice in a fantasy
is in fact a dream of mosquitoes chasing each other under sparks,
so many cities have fallen and been traded back.

Now the tree is once again called a Flame Tree
remaining luxuriant for heartless travelers,
but her ghost will never return here
The excuse is that it's had a most perfect ending
The extremely high wall can still be seen deep at night
The wind will not turn into a coiled dragon just because of the moonlight.


## Night Vigil at Xiao Hong's Graveside: Dai Wangshu

A long and lonely six-hour walk
This is the right spot for your grave
You are bashfully deceased
There are no more struggles, no more hatred
no words to write quatrains
You have come to sit like a pipe.

Night air has coagulated, the entire world's come here
and become part of the dark night
You are sitting amongst it all, because of red mountain tea

而成為了黑夜的中心
短暫地成為了黑夜的中心
像徒步穿越十九世紀的荷爾德林。

你也曾經是趕路的信使
一路上和自己的寂寞辯駁
以至無語，信已經封緘
蓋著時代火紅的大印
實在無法讓你說得更多
你的馬也不是不知疲倦的羅西南德。

誰在臥聽海濤閒話
空置的、人的家室中松針落下
夜氣清明，全世界卻都撤離
泳灘上閃著磷光
老魚吹浪如像地圖上所繪那樣
遠處空出了救生員的位置。

你來到這裏坐下，像一把煙斗
連寫一首四行詩的字詞都沒有了
戰爭沒有了，怨恨沒有了
你是羞澀的逝者
這裏適合做你的墓地
走六小時寂寞的長途。

You have become the dark night's center,
the temporary center of the dark night
like walking across nineteenth-century Hölderlin.

You were once a hurried messenger
on the road, in dispute with your loneliness
until there were no words left, the letters already
stamped with the bright red official seal of the era;
I really cannot let you say any more,
it's not like your horse is the indefatigable Rocinante.

Lying down and listening to the gossip of great waves
pine needles are falling on somebody's unused home
Night air is bright, yet the entire world is scattered
at the beach, fish scales sparkle
old fish blow waves like those drawn on a map
far off the life guard's seat has been vacated.

You've come here to sit like a pipe
There are no more words for quatrains
No more struggles, no more hatred
You are bashfully deceased
This is the right spot for your grave
A long and lonely six-hour walk.

# 聖誕書，或黑童話

——為劉曉波先生而作

大霧彌蓋了伶仃洋海面，超過
八艘船相撞。昨天北方降溫、
西南的飛機暫停升降，明天香港
也將氣溫急降。這個耶誕節
沒有更多的新聞，像染劑噬入我的血管
為一場手術前觀察造影，
除了這一場疼痛：病死的軟組織
把活生生的喉管勒緊。

大霧中有人跣足行於水面，
我不知道他的名字但我大聲叫喊——
一隻戴著蛇皮手套的手捂住了一把血塊
另一隻手趕緊檢索我的箭衣和帛袋
第三隻手摸出了我的酷熱和凜寒
第四隻手摘除了我的子宮
第五隻手敲開我的膝蓋
第六隻手埋進一條魚。

黑暗嘯聚。灰色馬，汗水蜿蜒
變成一條滾燙的河流，
我被棄於此——頭顱整好垂下渴飲。
現實中有人擰匙開門、生火煮茶……
一陣陣大火把他們的生活一陣陣利索收拾了。
柳條兒飄、春水俏，另一個世界
顛簸沉落——喜鵲啄啄
我的眼眶裡有明珠一串，你拽得動否？

# A Christmas Book, or Dark Fairy Tale

*—A Poem for Liu Xiaobo*

Thick fog covers the Lingding sea, surpassing
the collision of eight ships. Yesterday's temperature dropped in the north,
in the southwest all air travel was cancelled, tomorrow in Hong Kong
the temperature also will fall sharply. This Christmas
there will be no more news like dyes biting into my blood vessels
to read the angiogram before the operation,
except for this pain: the soft tissue dies of illness
strangling the trachea alive.

In the thick fog someone walks barefoot on the water,
I don't know his name but I shout loudly—
a hand in snakeskin gloves muffles a clot
another hand hastily searches my armor and silk bag
the third detects my intense heat and cold
the fourth plucks my womb
the fifth breaks my knee
the sixth buries a fish

They gather in the dark. Grey horses, sweat writhes
and turns into a boiling river,
I am abandoned here—my head is neat and hangs down, I am dying of thirst.
In reality someone opens the door with a key, makes a fire and tea . . .
Large fires put their lives in precise order,
willows sway, spring water is good, another world
jolts and sinks—magpies peck
a string of pearls in my eyes, can you drag it out?

誰是夜裡動身上路人？嗚嗚
我送他一陣風、一掛雪、一本前朝敘亡帖。
現在的能見度只有半米，但我知道
你能聽辨碎步踩響瓦當、矮身
就跟上了房頂，你掏出一瓶烈酒
我就輸給你我的半生，
你伸手，便會看見這肝膽歷歷
盡可做你的刀槍。

大霧搪塞著我的行囊
咄咄，咄咄，不是敲門，是幽靈
在給我照相。像酒鬼把人行道卷起來
我把路打了結，把地球裹成聖誕禮物，
送給他：他在地上畫字，一言不發，
他的弟子全部不敢靠攏，儘管天大寒、
來日大難，儘管及目都是髑髏地
他撿起了一朵白色花。

Who is leaving at night? Boo hoo
I hand him a gust of wind, a piece of snow, a notice of the previous
                    dynasty's demise.
Now visibility is only half a meter, but I know
you can make out the sound of steps on roof tiles, short bodies
follow me up on the roof, you pull out a liquor bottle,
I lose half my life to you,
reaching out your hands you can see the heroic spirit and courage
daring to become your weapons.

Thick fog becomes a fence for my luggage,
tut tut, there's no knocking on the door, it's a spectre
taking photos of me. Like a drunkard rolling up the sidewalk
I knotted the road and wrapped the world like a Christmas present
to offer it to him: he's writing on the ground, not saying a word,
none of his disciples dare come closer, in spite of the weather,
disaster is nearing, he picks a white flower in spite of the Place of the Skull
right in front of our eyes.

# 影的告別

"在支離的樹影上，我看見一個少年的影子前行。他的兩肩寬闊，腰板堅直，像穿了宇宙船駕駛員的制服，遨遊於一九九一年，不知道宇宙將凝結爲一渾濁磨花的玻璃球、衆星壓叠如濕重的枯葉。

"他擺動雙臂彷彿有阿童木的猛力，把十多年的淤泥嘩啦啦撥開，如劍魚劈開血海，他劈開一九九三年的囚獄、一九九七年的流放、一九九九年的瘋癲、二零零三年的窒息、二零零五年的二零零八年的二零一零年的死亡。他一握若脆的手腕，竟綁了一艘油輪的駕重。

"樹影劃過那些軋軋作響的骨骼，黑暗爲我們身邊一切蒙上一張巨大的驢皮，冰涼且腥。我們在全然看不見對方的時候握手道別，我爲他點了一根煙，順勢把他背上全部的負荷挾爲己有。在如銀河一樣熄滅的火雨之路上，他有他的、我有我的一葉舟。"

我和一個騎著馬骸的孩子說了這個寓言，他並不認爲這是個寓言，踢著我的頭骨，他又邀四周的小鴇們開始了新的遊戲。

# A Shadow's Farewell

"Upon the shattered shadow of a tree, I watched a youth's shadow step forward. His shoulders were broad, his back was straight, looking like an astronaut roaming through 1991, not knowing the universe would coagulate into a frosted glass ball, stars stacking like wet withered leaves.

"He waved his arms with the vigor of Astro Boy, pushing aside in a crashing sound mud that had silted up over a decade, like a swordfish splitting a sea of blood, he split the prison of 1993, the exile of 1997, the lunacy of 1999, the suffocation of 2003, the death of 2010 of 2008 of 2005. Once he clenched his brittle wrists, he eventually could bear the weight of an oil tanker.

"The shadow of a tree paddled over grinding bones and skeletons, darkness draped over everything around us with an enormous beast's skin, cold and rank. We shook hands and said goodbye when we were unable to see each other anymore I lit a cigarette for him, and then heaved the burden from his back onto mine. Rain on the road along the Milky Way that looked like an extinguished fire, he had his small boat, and I had mine."

I told this fable to a child riding the skeleton of a horse, but he didn't consider it a fable, kicking at my skull, he invited the little owls around him to play a new game.

# 紀念一位我素未謀面的詩人

秦王啊缺席如刺客。而我，像那
胖子，朝遍地的天意再三鞠躬
——張棗《醉時歌》

"保護刺客！有皇上！"
先講一個段子，一個中國段子。

傳說中你常醉，且哭，
一桌子珍饈也哭。嘩一聲你掀翻了北京。

聰明山、豔麗湖，在在都是野心，
歲月五花大綁，朝黑暗喊：放人！

一筷子一筷子，你吃著她，她
吃著你。牡丹們安排了宴席，火燒夜

不是在圖賓根。你身上的木匠揮汗
彷彿斫冰在北海深處，你身上的死亡師傅。

為全世界，你不認識漢語以外的語言。
你沉默，沉默是一個中國段子。

海開門吧，筆尖折斷了一艘戰列艦，
你用沙盤推演了一場從未發生的大戰。

寂靜的床榻下面，鬼在敲門，
你說你學習了上海主義，阿拉不是白相人。

# In Memory of a Poet I Never Met

*Oh, King of Qin, absent as an assassin. And me, like the*
*fat guy, bow three times in all directions before the Will of Heaven*

—Zhang Zao, "Song Sung When Drunk"

"Protect the assassin! The Emperor is coming!"
First telling a joke, a Chinese joke.

In the legend you were always drunk, and crying,
even with a table full of delicacies you cried. Your clanging stirred Beijing.

Clever mountain, beautiful lake, ambition is everywhere,
times are trussed up, shouting to the dark: release me!

Chopstick by chopstick, you eat her, she
eats you. Peonies arrange a banquet, a burning night.

Not in Tübingen. The carpenter in you is sweating
Like hoeing ice in the North Sea's depths, with the death master in you.

To the whole world, you know no other language than Chinese.
You are silent, silence is a Chinese joke.

Sea, open the door, a pen nib has broken a battleship,
you plan a military mission for a war that never happens.

Under a quiet bed, ghosts are knocking at the door,
you say you have learnt Shanghai-ism, I am not a hooligan.

啊這些鬼、這些鬼壘起了外白渡橋，
你箭步如簫，摸著了彤雲的屁股。

我知道有一晚中國大霧，嚓嚓迸裂著丘陵和皮膚；
那些沒有影子的人，雙腳離地有一尺之遙。

一本詩集只剩下了十四行。你一邊撕
我一邊燒。火鍋裏浮沉著龍的大多數。

儂吃儂吃！你就是那個刺客吧？
到處都是朝廷，到處都是皇上，到處都是尖叫。

Oh those ghosts, those ghosts built the Garden Bridge,
you run as fast as a blown bamboo flute, and touch the butt of rosy clouds.

I know that one night there was a thick fog in China, that screeched open
              the hills and skins;
Those people with no shadows, their feet one foot off the ground.

Only fourteen lines left in a collection of poems. While you're shredding
I burn them. The majority of dragons float in a hot-pot.

You eat you eat! Are you the assassin?
The imperial court is everywhere, the emperor is everywhere, screaming
              is everywhere.

# 一九四九

讓我回到我出生二十六年前，
四海陰霾，白沫如咒寫滿天幕，
我危立在一朵黑浪上，一千萬粗糲的
餓鬼穿過我的空殼左右來往。

我冷，我冷，毛澤東壓根沒有見過馬克思
只抱著一個豔麗的阿鼻地獄就下了山；
我冷，我冷，蔣介石壓根沒有見過耶和華
只抱著一個描金的閻羅就過了江。

竹子林裏下著雨，我們觸著，儘是火焰……
靴子裏開了花，伸腳進去呢，儘是碎骨……
你不知道人的骨頭多大多脆吧？
甚至每一隻粉蝶都載一朵霹靂的叫聲。

讓我回到我父十四歲，臉上怒放幼虎的紋
很快就被四方射來的血箭洗清。
我危立在一朵黑浪上，接不住這未生之國、
這亂拋於狂風之末的一個少年。

# 1949

Let me go back twenty-six years before I was born,
the four seas hazy, white foam like a curse written across the heavens,
I stand precariously on a black wave, ten million rough
hungry ghosts pass back and forth over my empty shell.

I am cold, so cold. Mao Zedong never saw Marx
carrying just a flowery Avici he came down from the mountains;
I am cold, so cold. Chiang Kai-shek never saw Yahweh
carrying just a gilded Yama, he crossed the river.

It is raining in the bamboo forest, when we touch it, they are all flames . . .
Flowers opened in boots, we push our feet in, inside is all broken bones . . .
Don't you know how big and brittle human bones are?
Even white butterflies carry the blossom of a thundering cry.

Let me go back to when my father was fourteen, the lines of his face
                    blooming like a tiger cub.
They will soon be washed away by bloody arrows shot from everywhere.
I stand precariously on a black wave, unable to catch this unborn country,
this youth, hastily discarded at the end of chaos.

## 霧中作

維多利亞港的霧已經含混近乎謠言，
吞吐大荒，但船仍在來往，
拖船、渡輪、豪華遊船、駁船、漁舟，
都是海底入睡的淤泥大王吐出的點點逗號，
霧匍伏著爬過海面，和小浪花繾綣
輕輕地又交換了舞伴，微笑著
微笑又漠然，爬上潮濕的金紫荊廣場，
舌頭伸進了遊人嘴，手探進了其褲腰，
霧沿著海堤摟緊了中銀大廈、國際金融中心等等，
他的臉蹭著香港的重重黑幕、隔夜茶色玻璃，
閃著一個個媚眼，他閃過灣仔運動場
恨恨地繞了一圈一圈，巨大的沉默在將他抵擋，
我幾乎聽到他因為失戀而哭，
人民不愛他，我也不愛他，
但我在新鴻基中心三十三樓空空的辦公室裏召喚他，
過來，過來，我的心能容下這一場毒霧，
我彷彿聽見每一個絕望的人民也都這樣召喚。

# Written in Fog

The fog over Victoria Harbour is nearly as ambiguous as rumor,
which handles an overgrown universe, but vessels come and go,
tugboats, ferries, luxury liners, barges and fishing dorries,
dots and commas spit out by the King of Sludge sleep at the bottom of the sea,
as the fog creeps over the sea, intimate with the surge,
gently trading dance partners, smiling and
yet indifferent, climbing on the damp Golden Bauhinia Square,
tongue thrust into tourists' mouths, hand stretched into their waistbands,
on the embankment the fog embraces the Bank of China Tower, the IFC,
                    and on,
rubbing his face against all the black curtains and overnight tea shaded glass
                    of Hong Kong,
making eyes at all of them, flashing over the Wan Chai Sports Ground,
wickedly coiling about it, a great silence blocking him,
and I can almost hear him cry in heartache,
the people do not love him, I do not love him either,
but in an empty office on the thirty-third floor of the Sun Hung Kai Centre
                    I call him,
come here, come here, my heart can take this toxic mist,
I seem to hear the same cries from all the desperate people.

# 失蹤者

——為艾未未等被失蹤者而坐

三十個小時了，你在尋找我們。
三十天了，三十年了，
一位，無數位失蹤的人在尋找我們，
你們在山壑，莽原，河床留下足印，標下記號，
標出我們作為一個人的形狀，標出一個
國度作為人自由呼吸的空間的形狀，
磅礴如你們空出來的位置，鼓滿了新雪。

此刻我們吃飯就是練習你的饑餓，
此刻我們入睡就是成為你的夢境，
此刻我們醒來就是代替你在說話，用消失的嘴巴，
而我們說話就是吐出你嘴裡的血塊，我們吐出
血塊就是向大風擊拳，我們擊拳就是為了證明
我們的存在，我們存在是為了
反駁虛無的無所不能。

日子從紅走到黑，又從黑走到黃，
烏鴉照舊梳頭海豹照舊做愛，人照舊擁有人的名字，
但在回頭時發現那個留下來佇立的自己已經不見了，
那個留下來和一堵牆辯論的自己被牆的陰影吞沒了，
那個嘗試把陰影卷起來放到郵包裡的自己被收繳了，
那個被擦去了收件人地址的自己被放進了碎紙機，
碎片各自拿著一個鋒利的偏旁。

# The Missing

*—to Ai Weiwei, and others "forced to disappear" in China*

It's been thirty hours and you are looking for us.
Thirty days, thirty years,
one, countless missing people are searching for us,
you left your footprints in the hills, the bushes, the riverbeds,
in the shape of a human figure,
in the shape of a country where people can breathe freely,
as vast as the void left by your absence, filled with newly fallen snow.

Now we eat just to practice your hunger,
now we sleep just to become your dream,
now we wake just to speak for you, with missing mouths
and to speak is to spit the blood clot in your mouth,
to spit the blood clot is to shake our fists at the blustery wind
to shake our fists is to prove our existence
and to exist is to deny
the omnipotence of nothingness.

Days changed from red to black, from black to yellow,
still, crows comb their hair while seals make love, people own their names,
but as they looked back they found their standing selves had disappeared,
the selves who'd stayed to debate with a wall swallowed by the wall's shadow,
the selves who attempted to roll up the shadows into a parcel confiscated,
the selves who had their recipients' addresses erased put through a shredder,
each shred of paper carrying a sharp fragment of word.

我們僅餘偏旁，頓挫，曲折，支離。我們是白樺樹
滿身是昨日的抗議，抗議已經成為一首詩。
讓冰刀在樹的夢境裡一推到底，
讓馬兒低頭看見水面上銀箔似的蹄印……
早起的步行者們如群馬在晨霧中消失，
霧也試探邁開四蹄躊躇如未生之國，
它仍在我們當中尋找騎手。

We are left with fragments of words, rises and falls, twists and turns,
           disintegration. We are the birch.
Yesterday's protests are written across my body, the protests became a poem.
Let the ice saw cut all the way into the tree's dream,
let the horse look at its own footprints on the water like silver foil . . .
the stroller who rose up early disappeared into the mist like horses,
the mist attempted to stride with its staggering hooves like an unborn nation,
still searching for riders among us.

# 毋祭文

——致西藏自焚者

一團又一團火像冰凍的星籟籟熄滅
沒有甚麼，大地上只剩我們未被燃點

死亡不是詩的理由，再生也不是
星星的殘骸落在雪中，刹那十萬年

十萬度高溫的凝凍物，這黑晶
是我們稱之為鳳凰的，你們稱之為獅子

在我們十四億人的虛空上淒喚的水晶
在你們五百萬人的戰意下低哮的水晶

這赤水中賓士的黑冰無從加持
閃電雲層中逃逸的離子靈魂無從挾持

只剩我們了，未被燃點未曾詛咒和圓滿
危石累累曲趾拳拳抱卵如未生

一團又一團星雲無知於你們我們
以彼此愛恨為酒輪迴路上一醉的死者

# An Elegy That Does Not Mourn

*for self-immolation victims in Tibet*

fireballs flashed into darkness like frozen stars
nothing else is left, we are the only ones not burnt on this planet

death is not the reason for poetry, nor rebirth
the wreckage of stars fell on snow, a hundred thousand years flew by
                              in a split second

crystallized in one hundred thousand degrees, this black crystal
we call a phoenix, you call a lion

a crystal that weeps atop an emptiness of 1.4 billion
a crystal that growls beneath the fighting will of five million people

black ice that gallops in scarlet water can't be granted the jinlab's blessing
an ionic soul that flees from lightning clouds can't be taken hostage

we are the only ones not yet ignited or cursed or enlightened
as rugged cliff as gnarled toes as hugging an egg as if unborn

all those nebulae know nothing of you, and we
are the dead on the road to reincarnation, drunk with liquor made from each
                              other's love and hate

# 擬末日詩

——給疏影

最後一班航機
在七點準起飛
漸漸進入永恆
這個彆扭名字
那死神的面具
這靈蛇的首尾

淨化開始發生
烈焰像綠葉海
舔舐乾旱洪荒
那些光輝燦爛
的人類紀念碑
不必等我重回
就簽署了腐蝕
浪花另一身姿

不須十五分鐘
天已經黑得連
黑夜也看不見
但是親愛的你
看那乾脆的花
那些瑟瑟靈魂
搖擺如這星球
最原始的一夏

# Drafting a Doomsday Poem

*—for Shuying*

The last flight departs
7 o'clock sharp
slowly entering eternity
this awkward name
that mask of Death
a quick snake's head and tail

The purification process begins
in raging flames like a green sea
licking drought from primeval times
those glorious and magnificent
monuments of mankind
need not wait for my return
to sign up the corrupt episodes
of life for another appearance

In less than fifteen minutes
it turns so dark that even
the night can't be seen
but you my dear
looks at that clear-cut flower
those trembling souls that
swing like one of this planet's
most primitive summers

我們飛機懸浮
平流層的銀光
利刃翩翩之中
離毀滅隔千山
距重生猶千海
靜靜地看文明
閉合薔薇花蕾
親愛的你看那
億萬雄雌花蕊
烈焰當中交配

待冷落再重來
鯨骨下新家宅
將為不存在的
你我遮蔽裸日
為昨日水默寫
為沙之書檢索
為無字詩誦讀
為白矮星表演
輕盈尼金斯基

Our plane is floating
Silver rays from the stratosphere
dancing lightly amid sharp blades
a thousand mountains from destruction
a thousand seas from rebirth
quietly watching civilization
closing rose buds
my dear you watched those
millions of stamens and pistils
breeding in raging flames

When coldness comes back
a new home under a whalebone
will protect a non-existent you
and me from the naked sun
writ yesterday in water from memory
to find clues in books of sand
to recite poems without words
to perform for white dwarf stars
lithe and graceful as Nijinski

# 星空下

### I

我觀察到這兩個地球生物
在星空下他們的庇護所內
黑暗中遊戲，一大一小
長相酷似，似宇宙間極細的兩星球
互相環繞打轉
小的叫喚：baba，大的回應：chuchu
他們就這樣呢喃著沈入了睡眠狀態
像那些鏡子上的微光，落入黑水深處

### II

初初叫着爸爸睡著了
我也難抵沈重下潛到五潯的夢底下
死去二十六年的外公扶著牆壁走來
我上前攙扶他，他比死時強壯
依然是舊藍色工作服圍繞他如星空
我透過他能看見銀河傾斜了片刻
動盪如盆水馬上又平靜
他沒有死，夜夜歸來看
我們安眠，在星空下
時而輕輕抱我，如我抱你，入懷

150

# Under a Starry Sky

### I

I watch two living earthbound creatures
under the stars within their sanctuary
playing in the dark, one big one small
looking just the same, like two tiny stars in the universe
revolving around each other,
the small one shouted *baba*, the big one answered *chuchu*
They whispered like that, falling into a deep sleep
like glimmers on a mirror falling into the depths of black water

### II

Chuchu told baba to fall asleep
It's hard to sustain the heaviness of a dream five fathoms deep
Granddad who died twenty-six years ago touches the wall when he walks
I move forward to support him, he is stronger than when he died
The old blue uniform still revolves around him like a starry sky
I can see the Milky Way slanting through him for a moment
dangling like a tub of water, immediately returning to a standstill
He has not died, each night he returns
to see me sleep peacefully, sometimes beneath the starry
sky he holds me gently, like I hold you, in my arms

### III

爸爸　樹葉　貓咪
車車　燈　河　水
媽媽　星星　媽媽
嘩　嘩　嘩……
（星空下這些人和他們身上的塵埃
被星光照徹，他們感激死亡帶來安息，
而清晨寬宏，無數次如清水
重新灌滿他們的軀殼——
奧米迦，貝塔，迦瑪。）

III

Baba  tree-leaves  kittens
Cars  lamps  rivers  water
Mama  stars  mama
Blub blub blub . . . . . .
(These people under a starry sky, dust on their bodies
illuminated by starlight, grateful for the peace that death brings,
while mornings are magnanimous, immeasurable as clear water
that once again fills up their bodies—
Omega, Beta, Gamma.)

# Notes

### Tree outside the Window
Zhongguancan is a technological hub in Beijing's northwestern district that is known as China's Silicon Valley.

### Another Divining Cat Poem, on a Spring Night
The fruit of the elm tree resembles ancient Chinese copper coins, which share the same name.

### Charlie on Temple Street
A huadan is a female lead in traditional Chinese theatre (*Xiqu*).

### The Ballad of Queen's Pier
"Queen's Robber" is a song by the Hong Kong group Tat Ming Pair. In Cantonese the title is a play on Queen's Road.

"Ink family tree in Kowloon" is a reference to the late Tsang Tsou Choi, the King of Kowloon. He believed that most of Kowloon belonged to his ancestor, so he wrote his calligraphy on objects across Kowloon. One of the common calligraphic subjects was his family tree.

Another Tat Ming Pair song is "On that afternoon, I burned letters in my old house."

### The Future History of Hong Kong Island
Des Voeux and Johnston Roads are main streets on the northern side of Hong Kong Island that run through the Central and Western District. Both of them were built on reclamation land at different periods. Trams run along these roads.

HKCEC: abbreviation of the Hong Kong Convention and Exhibition Centre, which is located in the Wanchai district along Victoria Harbour.

International Finance Centre: abbreviated as IFC, is a skyscraper located in Central along Victoria Harbour.

North Point and Sai Ying Pun: early urban settlements on the northern side of Hong Kong Island.

Admiralty and Central: commercial districts on the northern side of Hong Kong Island.

Pandas are kept at the Ocean Park amusement complex in Wong Chuk Hang.

Cemetery clusters are located in Happy Valley and Chai Wan.

**In Beijing, I Watch a Documentary of the July 1 Hong Kong March**
Fuling District is located centrally in China's Chongqing Municipality.

**"After writing an anti-war poem I leave the house"**
A northwestern area of Lantau Island in Hong Kong, and the poet's home.

Ivan is the orphan from the 1962 Soviet movie Ivan's Childhood, directed by Andrei Tarkovsky.

**Fog: Taiping Shan Peak**
McDull: character from a popular Hong Kong children's cartoon.

Taiping Shan: Hong Kong's highest peak at 554 meters.

The Lingding Sea lies between Hong Kong and Macau, over which the Hong Kong-Zhuhai-Macau Bridge is being built.

Tianpeng is the name of a deity.

**Reading the Xinxing County Gazetteer**
Liu Waitong was born in Xinxing County.

Geliao: ancient name for ethnic minorities in South China.

### The Best of Times

The film title is usually translated as *Three Times*, but this does not connect the meaning of the title to the content of the poem.

Liang Qichao (1873–1929) was a brilliant Confucian scholar who worked to balance traditional Chinese culture and socio-political structures with democratic reforms.

Shu Qi was the lead actress in the movie *The Best of Times*.

Preta realm: domain of "Hungry Ghosts" in Mahayana Buddhism.

### In Time of Peace

A reflection of W. H. Auden's *In Time of War*.

The Memorial Hall commemorates those who lost their lives in the fight against the Japanese who invaded the north in 1931.

Literally "Grotto Court," Dongting lake in Hunan province is where the first dragon boat races were held.

The Miao minority is known for practicing witchcraft.

Pingyao: a county in Shanxi. The city is known for its well-preserved ancient features and is recognized as a UNESCO World Heritage Site.

Xu Xiake (1587–1641) was a well-known Chinese travel writer and geographer.

Xu Xiacun (1907–1986), Dai Wangshu (1905–1950) and Shi Zhecun (1905–2003) were all Chinese writers.

Jiangnan is an area south of the lower stretch of the Yangtze River.

Xishan, or Western hills, are the hills and mountains in the western part of Beijing. Shanyin is a district in Shanxi.

Han Yu (768–824), poet and essayist, is famous for his "Memorial on Buddha's bone," a protest against Buddhism. Han Bo is a modern poet.

Gao Shi (ca. 704–765) was a Tang poet. Gao Xiaotao is a modern poet and photographer.

In Theravada Buddhism, an "arhat" refers to a person who has reached a perfected state.

Wang Wei (699–759) was a Tang poet. Wang Wei is a modern writer.

Li He (790–816) was a Tang poet.

Bohai Sea or Bay is the inner gulf of the Yellow Sea located near Beijing.

Qiu Jin (1875–1907) was a late Qing revolutionary who was executed for her role in a failed uprising against the Qing Dynasty.

Huang Binhong (1865–1955) was a Chinese art historian and painter.

Su and Bai causeways cross the West Lake in Hangzhou and are named after the famous poets Su Dongpo (1037–1101) and Bai Juyi (772–847).

Taohua Island: literally Peach Blossom Island, is one of the islands of the Zhoushan archipelago. Wagang Camp is in Henan. It seems here to stand for the contrast between a peaceful island and a military stronghold.

Zhang Zhixin (1930–1975) was a dissident during the Cultural Revolution. She was imprisoned and executed for expressing views critical of the Communist Party. Liu Hezhen (1904–1926) died in the March 18 massacre, which originally began as a protest against unequal treaties between China and foreign countries, but ended in violence when military police forced the protesters to disperse. Xu Xilin (1873–1907) was part of the same failed uprising as Qiu Jin.

Xing Tian: a deity in Chinese mythology who continued to fight against the supreme god, even after being beheaded. Xing Tian stands as a symbol for perseverance.

The May 16 Notification was a text issued in 1966, in which Mao Zedong (1893–1976) gives an ideological justification for the Cultural Revolution.

Tao Chengzhang (1878–1912) was involved in revolutionary activities to overthrow the Qing Dynasty, along with Qiu Jin and Xu Xilin.

Ji Kang (223–262) was a poet, and composer. Zhang Zhou, better known as Zhuangzi (fl. 4th century BC), was a Taoist philosopher.

### Looking for Woodbrook Villa on Pokfulam Road

Poet's note: "Woodbrook Villa" was where Dai Wangshu lived in Hong Kong after 1938. It is located at 92a–92c Pokfulam Road on Hong Kong Island, near Pokfield Road.

Mount Davis: westernmost hill on Hong Kong Island.

Origin of the name "Pokfulam."

### Sonnet

Kumbum: Tibetan Buddhist monastery located in Qinghai.

### Revisiting Du Fu's Thatched Cottage

Du Fu's Thatched Cottage refers to the park and museum on the outskirts of Chengdu, built to commemorate the Tang Poet Du Fu (712–770).

Auntie Huangs refers to Du Fu's neighbor, who he writes about in his poem "Walking Alone by the Riverbank Seeking Flowers" (《江畔獨步尋花》).

### Poem for the Universe's Prostrating-Walk

Jingwei is a mythical bird that tries to fill the ocean with stones, and symbolizes futile ambition.

Mudra: symbolic gesture made in Hinduism and Buddhism.

### Jesus Is on Temple Street (A-yun's Christmas Song)

Poet's note: "Jesus is on Temple Street" is a large sign posted by religious groups on Temple Street.

### Luk Ming Street: To Madame Wu

Poet's note: Madame Wu is the widow of poet Tse Shan (謝山, 1922–1996),

who wrote Poems of Bitterness 《苦口詩詞草》. Madame Wu and poet Tse Shan both took part in the Trotskyist movement in China and were persecuted under the Maoist regime. Wu now lives in Hong Kong and has written a biography of Tse Shan (《詩人謝山傳》).

Maud Gonne (1866–1953) was an Irish revolutionary perhaps best known for her relationship with William Butler Yeats.

"Deer bleat loud [and] eat in the wild" (呦呦鹿鳴，食野之苹) is a direct quote from a poem in the *Book of Odes* 《詩經》 as well as "The Short Song" (〈短歌行〉) of Cao Cao (曹操) (155–220), the Chancellor of the Han Dynasty (206 BC–220 AD). Here it is also a reference to the street name, Luk Ming Street, which literally means Deer Bleat Street.

"The moon is bright and stars are few" (月明星稀) is a direct quote from Cao Cao's "The Short Song".

### Register of Ghosts: Haizi

Haizi committed suicide along a stretch of railway near Qinhuangdao in Hebei province, close to where the Great Wall meets the ocean.

"Today I hear only tranquil gunshots" is a reference to the June Fourth massacre in Tiananmen Square.

An obtuse reference to the motion of troops through Beijing during June Fourth, replacing Muxidi, the site of the earliest real violence, with Muxudi, a "field of clover," and Xizhimen with different characters.

### Register of Ghosts: Luo Yihe

*Register of Ghosts* by Zhong Sicheng (c. 1279–1360) is a book written in the 14th century. It contains the history and stories of several Yuan dynasty Qu poets. The title of the book literally reads "a record of ghosts" and individuals have used this title to refer both to departed people and ghosts. Here, Liu uses it as a title for people who died as part of the June Fourth movement.

**1967, May Fourth Memorabilia**
The poem was written after reading Zhi An's biography of Zhou Zuoren, and is about Zuoren and his elder brother Lu Xun.

Fei Lian and Qiong Qi: demonic beasts from Chinese mythology.

Literally "Red Capital," which refers to Yan'an in Shaanxi, is where the communists established their headquarters in 1936.

Pseudonym of Miyatake Kameshiro (1867–1955), a Japanese writer who advocated equality for all. His idea was to abolish surnames, but that was not practical for household registration. Therefore Miyatake used his pen name Haisei Gaikotsu, which translates roughly as "nameless outerbones."

**A Seaside Graveyard: Three Poems**
Xiao Hong (1911–1942), Dai Wangshu (1905–1950) and Eileen Chang (Zhang Ailing 1920–1995) are all Chinese writers.

Hulan: district in Harbin where Xiao Hong was born.

Poet's note: Some of Xiao Hong's ashes were buried at the Seaside Garden, Repulse Bay, and relocated to Guangzhou in 1957. Part of Zhang Ailing's story *Love in a Fallen City* takes place at the Repulse Bay Hotel, Hong Kong. Dai Wangshu went to visit Xiao Hong's grave in 1944 and wrote the famous lines "Impromptu Verse at Xiao Hong's Graveside."

**In Memory of a Poet I Never Met**
The poet Zhang Zao (1962–2010).

The Waibaidu Bridge in Shanghai, also known as the Garden Bridge, was China's first all steel bridge.

**1949**
*1949* is a collection of historical essays by Lung Ying-tai, published in 2009.

# Translation Acknowledgments

**Enoch Yee-lok Tam**
Tree outside the Window
Another Diving Cat Poem, on a Spring Night
A Song of Spring Light
4am, Make Love to Me
Charlie on Temple Street
In Beijing, I Watch a Documentary of the July 1 Hong Kong March
"After writing an anti-war poem I leave the house"
Fog, Taiping Shan Peak
Reading the Xinxing County Gazetteer
The Best of Times
Ballad of Disheartenment
Register of Ghosts: Haizi
Register of Ghosts: Luo Yihe
Register of Ghosts: You
1967, May Fourth Memorabilia
A Seaside Graveyard: Three Poems
      In Front of a Grave: Xiao Hong
      A Stage for *Love in a Fallen City*: Eileen Chang
A Christmas Book, or Dark Fairy Tale
A Shadow's Farewell
In Memory of a Poet I Never Met
1949

# Author and Translator Bios

LIU Waitong is a poet, writer and photographer. He was born in Guangdong in 1975 and moved to Hong Kong in 1997. In 2001, Liu went to Beijing where he lived for five years before returning to Hong Kong. He has been awarded several literary prizes in Hong Kong and Taiwan, including the China Times Literary Award, the United Daily News Award, and the Hong Kong Arts Development Award for Best Artist (Literature). He often receives invitations to participate in local and international literary events, including the Taipei Poetry Festival in 2011 and Poetry International Rotterdam in 2013. Since his debut in 1995, Liu has published eleven collections of poetry, along with several books of critical essays and photography.

Desmond SHAM (b. 1984) studied Comparative Literature at the University of Hong Kong and has published poems and literary criticisms in journals and newspapers in Hong Kong and Taiwan. His poetry collection *dis-poetry* received the Recommended Prize in the 11th Hong Kong Biennial Awards for Chinese Literature.

Enoch Yee-Lok TAM (b. 1981) studied literature at the Hong Kong University of Science and Technology and now is a Ph.D. candidate, studying film at the Hong Kong Baptist University. He has published his first novel *The Happy Times of Blackeye* (黑目的快樂年代) in 2011 and is now an editor of the Hong Kong literary magazine *Fleurs des Lettres*.

Audrey HEIJNS received her MA in Chinese Studies from Leiden University and worked as Assistant Editor at *Renditions*, Chinese University of Hong Kong before joining the City University of Hong Kong as Research Fellow. She is a translator of Chinese poetry and prose, and editor of *VerreTaal*, the online database of Chinese literature in Dutch translation.

CHAN Lai-kuen graduated from the Chinese University of Hong Kong with a degree in English, and the Royal Melbourne Institute of Technology University (taken in Hong Kong) with a degree in fine art. Her book of poetry *Were the Singing Cats* (有貓在歌唱) was published in 2010. It was awarded the Recommendation Prize of the 11th Hong Kong Biennial Awards for Chinese Literature. She has participated in various literature and art crossover projects in Hong Kong and China.

CAO Shuying, born in Harbin, China, lives in Hong Kong. She is a poet and writer, who received her BA and MA in Chinese Literature from Peking University. She has published several poetry and essay collections, and has received a number of awards, including the Liu Li'an Poetry Prize, China Times' Literature Prize and the Hong Kong Biennial Award for Chinese Literature.